Interviewing a Professor of Finance: Basic Investments for Non-Professionals

Vol. 1 of the *Interviewing a Professor of Finance* Series

Huijian Dong, Ph. D., CFA

To my students who thrive to get the most out of their finance classes

To non-professional investors who need better capital return,
and thrive to learn reliable ways to get it

CONTENTS

ACKNOWLEDGMENTS

I greatly appreciate my students in the undergraduate and graduate classes, from the Business Administration major, Economics major, and Mathematics major, as well as the Master of Science in Finance program and the Master of Business Administration program at Pacific University, Oregon, USA. The courses through which they contributed to this book are: Business Finance, Personal Finance, Investments, Global Finance, Fixed-Income Asset Pricing, Modern Financial Instruments, Advanced Topics in Finance, Financial Management, Applied Investment Management, and Entrepreneurial Finance. The large amount of students attending different levels of higher education programs allows this book to deliver a thoroughly complete coverage of the standard questions about investments. Students' creative thoughts and sharp questions allow me to predict and address questions in the minds of the readers.

I am sincerely grateful to Professor Krishnan Ramaya, Professor John Suroviak, Professor Xiaomin Guo, Professor Phil Ruder, Professor Jamie Haag, Professor William Latham, Professor Helen Bowers, Professor Linhai Mei, Professor Yahua Zhao, and Professor Weiguo Dong for their dedicated advice and support in completing this book.

I am thankful for the research grant supported by Pacific University that has made it possible to bring this book into your hands. Ms. Patricia Coatney did a wonderful job in assisting the process.

As prestigious asset managers, Mr. Charles Nisker, CFA, and Mr. Ben James, CFA, contributed to the methods and insights suggested in this book. Without the help of my two dedicated editors, Ms. Katie Fairchild and Ms. Shannon Konoske, this book would not be smoothly delivered to the readers.

1 INTERVIEW STARTS

Stilleven Jobs just graduated from college. He is still looking for a job. He currently has $5,000 in savings and carries $40,000 in student loan debts. He plans to get married after eight years and become a father by that time. He wants to buy a house before his first kid is born, which will be about ten years from now. Aside from renting and cost of living, Stilleven does not have large expenditure commitments right now, but he wants to send "decent gifts" to his parents when he goes back home and visits them every Thanksgiving. Stilleven studied history at his undergraduate institution, and while he has absolutely no knowledge about investments, he is very willing to try. Stilleven's grandfather always told him, "control your own money, own control on your money."

    Wanna Buffet has just turned 35. She has large expenses on food, apparel, and her house. She is married and has three kids to feed: a six-year-old, a three-year-old, and a one-year-old. She has learned by now that "the terrible twos" does not just refer to two-year-olds, but in fact applies to kids between the ages of one and six. She has a very limited amount of time to deal with investments. The Buffets have a large amount of day-to-day living expenses. They still have a home mortgage of $300,000 and are planning to pay off the mortgage in the next twenty-six years. In the next twelve years, Wanna needs to save $50,000 for her older child's education. She wants to hire a financial advisor to invest for her family, yet she is wondering with their measly $2,000 monthly savings whether it is worth the hassle of hiring a finance professional to handle their investments.

    Baroque Omaha was married to **Moselle Omaha** but they are separated now. Baroque is taking care of their younger daughter who will attend college in two years. Baroque has no mortgage or other significant debt pressure. He would like to purchase a $115,000 piano for his daughter before she enters the music department at a famous college. Baroque has an unstable yet very well-paid job. He used to hire financial advisors to manage his investments, but he realized that there are years that his accounts incurred loss while his financial advisor still made money on top of earning a decent end-of-year bonus. Baroque now tries to invest on his own.

Moselle Omaha was married to **Baroque Omaha** but they are separated now. She has a stable job with a modest income. She is 55-years-old and plans to retire in no more than fifteen years. Now that her oldest daughter is married, Moselle's financial goal is to accumulate good savings to support a high quality lifestyle after she retires. She does not like investments, but she understands that they are important, so she forces herself to learn to manage her money.

Professor Dong's profile is presented at the end of this volume. Please refer to the page "About the author."

Professor Dong: Welcome to the first interview! There are three interview scripts published in the book series *Interviewing a Professor of Finance*, introduced as follows.

Volume One is necessary for understanding *Volume Two. Volume One* and *Two* work together to develop a reasonably complete, yet concise, knowledge set for non-professional equity investors. *Volume Three* can be a standalone investment guide for those interested in foreign exchange investments or currency investments.

The first interview script is presented in *Volume One* of the book series, which you hold in your hands. This book will discuss exchange-traded funds, investable assets for individuals, the insights of mutual funds, general investments planning, calculation, risk and reward self-evaluation, investment strategies, tactics, risk management, and options with their combinations.

The second interview script is presented in *Volume Two* of the book series, *Interviewing a Professor of Finance: Equity Investments for Non-Professionals*. It discusses the Economic analysis, industrial analysis, financial reports and how to make use the Yahoo! Finance resources to analyze a stock, chart reading and signaling analysis, portfolio management, and investor psychology. *Volume Two* also provides a detailed analysis of multiple diversification instruments that are commonly used: international equity, bond, private equity, real estate, insurance, and so on.

The third and final interview script is presented in *Volume Three* of the book series, titled *Interviewing a Professor of Finance: Currency Investments for Non-Professionals*. It first introduces and explains the foreign exchange market. *Volume Three* continues on to provide key suggestions and rules regarding currency investments. It discusses the chart reading and analysis skill, trading strategies, risk management, and the technique of trading on events. It also provides a list of common mistakes, drawn from experience and examples from tens of thousands of trades.

Here are some things to keep in mind about the interview:

The content of the interview is based on massive research results and conclusions cited from many authors, professors, researchers, and practitioners in the U.S. finance academia. In other words, this interview will not broadcast my personal view, personal experience, or what I personally learned from stock investments. This interview is a combination of the correct, reliable, and testable conclusions from both academia and the finance industry. It presents this combination as a doable and easily accessible manner in plain language.

The primary purpose of this interview is to make you understand how to scientifically, reasonably, and sustainably invest in the real U.S. stock market. I will present you with what is proved to be wrong, what is confirmed to be correct, and how to make investments in the real world.

There are hidden obstacles in the stock market that investors usually learn only after incurring their cost. This interview intends to map out these hidden obstacles before you experience them firsthand by running into them, so that you are not left to learn until after it's too late. For example, I will teach you how market price is ultimately random in the short run, a repeatedly examined conclusion from academia. This conclusion will help you avoid spending five years on chart reading and realize how useless that approach can be.

The investment opinions and suggestions introduced in this interview are neutral. During and before the interview, I do not directly or indirectly possess the assets under discussion. This interview is not sponsored by any financial institution. There is no undisclosed material conflict of interest.

Research conclusions and investment suggestions in this interview are based on historical data. As such, future market performance might not be consistent with these conclusions or suggestions. Theoretically-correct results may not be consistent with practical investments. If you follow the conclusions and suggestions in this book without adjusting to the dynamic market, you run the risk of losing your investment assets.

I strongly recommend that you take notes when reading this interview script. This is a serious discussion of the whole solution of investments, not a novel. I also recommend that you have access to the Internet and Microsoft Excel. This way, you the reader can practice investment analysis using web sources such as Yahoo! Finance, which is introduced in this book.

2 EXCHANGE-TRADED FUNDS

Wanna Buffet: So where do we start?

Professor Dong: Let's start by learning Exchange-Traded Funds, or ETF. This is an important asset class and we will need to frequently refer to it throughout this interview. So we learn it first before moving into introduction to investments.

If you don't have the first clue about investments and want to learn the big picture first, feel free to skip this chapter and read Chapter Three. Once you finish, come back and revisit this chapter.

Stilleven Jobs: What's an ETF? Why it is such an important type of asset?

Professor Dong: An Exchange-Traded Fund (ETF) is a basket of assets that investors can buy or sell as a single asset. For example, the ticker[1] of the most widely-traded ETF is SPY. This ETF attempts to mimic the return and performance of Standard and Poor's 500 index. One share of SPY includes 505 different stocks; among those stocks, the top holdings are 3.26% of Apple return, 2.46% of Microsoft return, 1.8% of Exxon Mobile return, and so on.

What this means is that if, for example, SPY is now traded at $200 per share, then buying 1 share of SPY is equivalent to paying $6.52 ($200, the cost of each share, multiplied by 3.26%, the percentage of Apple return) to buy a "piece" of Apple stock. This also means paying $4.92 (again, $200, the cost of each share, multiplied by 2.46%, the percentage of Microsoft return) to buy a "piece" of Microsoft stock.

Smart as you are, you might have already realized the advantages of trading ETFs.

---

[1] Ticker is the symbol of an asset that people use for convenience in the trading process. For example, the ticker of Walmart is WMT.

First, it provides you with low cost diversification. You can easily spend the price of one share of stock to set up a portfolio that includes many different assets. You do not need to have six figures on your account to buy 500 different stocks to diversify your portfolio to reduce the risk.

Second, the transaction cost is low. In the previous case, you pay one round-trip commission[2] to buy and sell one share of SPY, which is equivalent to buying and selling 505 different stocks. However, if you buy and sell the stocks individually, you need to pay the round-trip commission 505 times.

Third, trading ETFs allows you to have access to markets that are generally not accessible by individual investors, such as preferred stocks, bonds, or hedge funds. These assets are usually not traded at the secondary market with a high liquidity. These assets also have fairly high minimum entry requirements.

ETFs save tremendous time for non-professional investors who use passive investment strategies to track the market index. ETFs make trading indexes become possible. Prior to the development of ETFs, investors used to buy or sell representative stocks in anticipation of a market soar or plunge.

Ultimately, ETFs introduce investors to new asset areas without requiring those investors to do homework on individual assets. For example, investors interested in putting money into the New Zealand economy can buy an ETF named ENZL and ride out the country's booming economy. These investors don't need to look into the New Zealand stock market and investigate every single stock available to them.

In fact, there are ETFs for almost every topic: Brazilian small-cap stock, Japanese corporate junk bonds, the United States media industry, the global coffee market, etc. It's safe to say that there is almost always an ETF ready for you for whatever investment theme you are interested in.

Baroque Omaha: But what is a theme? Can you give us a complete list of ETF themes and the representative ETFs? I would like to refer to your list so I could reap the benefits of ETFs.

Professor Dong: This is a very good idea.

A theme is a topic or category where ETFs and stocks share common features. Some example themes include large U.S. stock, high dividend stock, and crude oil-related stock.

The following are representative ETFs that serve as a sector index, sector representative, or theme representative cited from etfdb.com. This list can also be found at the website etfdb.com.

---

[2] When you buy some shares of a stock, you pay commission to the broker. When you later sell them, you need to pay commission again. This is called the round-trip commission. A buy and a sell commission usually cost \$14 to \$18 in total.

ETF Sector, Industry, or Theme: All Cap Equities
Companies or entities included in the ETF: Invest in U.S. equities of all market capitalizations, or size – small cap, mid cap or large cap stocks.

Representative ETFs:
VTI

Expense ratio: 0.05%. Expense ratio is the cost of the ETF charged by the company that develops and maintains it. It will be deducted from your return.

VTI replicates the CRSP US Total Market Index. Over 4,000 constituents across mega, large, small and micro capitalizations, representing nearly 100% of the U.S. investable equity market, comprise the CRSP US Total Market Index.

USMV

Expense ratio: 0.15%

USMV replicates the MSCI USA Minimum Volatility Index, which aims to reflect the performance characteristics of a minimum variance strategy applied to the U.S. large and mid-cap equity universe. The USMV is calculated by optimizing the MSCI USA Index, its parent index, for the lowest absolute risk within a given set of constraints. Historically, the index has shown lower beta and volatility characteristics relative to the MSCI USA Index.

IWV

Expense ratio: 0.20%

IWV replicates the Russell 3000 Index, which is capitalization-weighted and consists of the 3,000 largest companies domiciled in the U.S. and its territories.

ETF Sector, Industry, or Theme: Alternative Energy Equities
Companies or entities included in the ETF: Invest in alternative energy companies that focus on solar, wind, hydroelectric, and geothermal energies.

Representative ETFs:
TAN

Expense ratio: 0.70%

TAN replicates the MAC Global Solar Energy Index, which is designed to track companies within the following business segments of the solar energy industry: solar power equipment and products for end-users, fabrication products or services for solar power equipment producers, raw materials or components, solar power system sales, distribution, installation, integration or financing, and selling electricity derived from solar power.

PBW

Expense ratio: 0.70%

PBW replicates the WilderHill Clean Energy Index, which is designed to deliver capital appreciation through the selection of companies that focus on green and renewable sources of energy, as well as technologies that facilitate clean energy.

GEX

Expense ratio: 0.62%

GEX replicates the Ardour Global Index, which provides exposure to publicly traded companies worldwide that are principally engaged in the alternative energy industry.

ICLN

Expense ratio: 0.47%

ICLN replicates the S&P Global Clean Energy Index, which measures the performance of global companies that represent the listed clean energy universe.

QCLN

Expense ratio: 0.60%

QCLN replicates the NASDAQ Clean Edge Green Energy Index, which is a modified market capitalization-weighted index designed to track the performance of clean energy companies that are publicly traded in the United States.

ETF Sector, Industry, or Theme: Asia Pacific Equities
Companies or entities included in the ETF: Invest primarily in companies based in the Asia-Pacific region, especially in Hong Kong, South Korea, and Japan.

Representative ETFs:
EWY

Expense ratio: 0.62%

EWY replicates the MSCI Korea Index, which measures the performance of the South Korean equity market.

VPL

Expense ratio: 0.12%

VPL replicates the FTSE Developed Asia Pacific Index, which consists of approximately 836 common stocks of companies located in Japan, Australia, South Korea, Hong Kong, Singapore, and New Zealand.

AAXJ

Expense ratio: 0.69%

AAXJ replicates the MSCI All Country Asia excluding Japan Index, which measures the performance of eleven developed and emerging equity markets.

EWT
Expense ratio: 0.62%
EWT replicates the MSCI Taiwan Index, which measures the performance of the Taiwanese equity market.

EPP
Expense ratio: 0.49%
EPP replicates the MSCI Pacific excluding Japan Index, which measures the performance of the Australian, Hong Kong, New Zealand, and Singapore equity markets.

EWA
Expense ratio: 0.49%
EWA replicates the MSCI Australia Index, which measures the performance of the Australian equity market.

ETF Sector, Industry, or Theme: Building & Construction
Companies or entities included in the ETF: Invest in homebuilder and construction companies.

Representative ETFs:
ITB
Expense ratio: 0.43%
ITB replicates the Dow Jones U.S. Select Home Construction Index, which measures the performance of the home construction sector of the U.S. equity market.

XHB
Expense ratio: 0.35%
XHB replicates the S&P Homebuilders Select Industry Index, which is the equal-weighted market cap homebuilding sub-industry portion of the S&P Total Markets Index.

ETF Sector, Industry, or Theme: China Equities
Companies or entities included in the ETF: Invest in China-based corporations.

Representative ETFs:
FXI
Expense ratio: 0.74%

FXI replicates the FTSE China 25 Index, which measures the performance of the largest companies in the China equity market.

GXC

Expense ratio: 0.59%

GXC replicates the S&P China BMI Index, which is a market capitalization-weighted index that defines and measures the investable universe of publicly traded companies that are domiciled in China but legally available to foreign investors.

MCHI

Expense ratio: 0.62%

MCHI replicates the MSCI China Index, which measures the performance of large cap Chinese equities.

EWH

Expense ratio: 0.49%

EWH replicates the MSCI Hong Kong Index, which measures the performance of the Hong Kong equity market.

ETF Sector, Industry, or Theme: Commodity Producers Equities
Companies or entities included in the ETF: Invest in companies that produce commodities such as gold miners, oil & gas, and agriculture products.

Representative ETFs:
GDX

Expense ratio: 0.53%

GDX replicates the NYSE Arca Gold Miners Index, which provides exposure to publicly traded companies worldwide that are involved in gold mining and is a diversified blend of stocks at different sizes.

GUNR

Expense ratio: 0.48%

GUNR replicates the Morningstar Global Upstream Natural Resources Index, which reflects the performance of a selection of equity securities that are traded in various markets, including the U.S. The business focuses on natural resources in energy, agriculture, precious or industrial metals, timber, and water resource sectors.

GDXJ

Expense ratio: 0.57%

GDXJ replicates the Market Vectors Global Junior Gold Miners Index, which provides exposure to a global universe of publicly traded small- and medium-capitalization companies that focus on gold and silver mining.

IGE

Expense ratio: 0.47%

IGE replicates the S&P North American Natural Resources Sector Index, which measures the performance of U.S.-traded natural resource-related stocks.

MOO

Expense ratio: 0.55%

MOO replicates the DAX global Agribusiness Index, which provides exposure to publicly traded companies worldwide that derive at least 50% of their revenues from the agriculture business.

GNR

Expense ratio: 0.40%

GNR replicates the S&P Global Natural Resources Index, which is comprised of the largest publicly traded companies in global natural resources and commodities businesses.

XME

Expense ratio: 0.35%

XME replicates the S&P Metals & Mining Select Industry Index, which is an equal-weighted market cap index.

WOOD

Expense ratio: 0.47%

WOOD replicates the S&P Global Timber & Forestry Index, which measures the performance of companies engaged in the ownership, management, or upstream supply chain of forests and timberlands.

CUT

Expense ratio: 0.70%

CUT replicates the Beacon Global Timber Index, which includes global timber companies.

ETF Sector, Industry, or Theme: Communications Equities
Companies or entities included in the ETF: Invest in companies in the communications sector, including telecommunications and media companies.

Representative ETFs:
IXP

Expense ratio: 0.47%

IXP replicates the S&P Global Telecommunications Sector Index, which measures the performance of the global telecommunications market.

XTL

Expense ratio: 0.35%

XTL replicates the S&P Telecom Select Industry Index, which represents the telecommunications sub-industry portion of the S&P Total Stock Market Index.

VOX

Expense ratio: 0.12%

VOX replicates the MSCI US Investable Market Telecommunication Services 25/50 Index, which includes firms at different cap size and provides communications services primarily through a fixed-line, cellular, wireless, high bandwidth, and/or fiber-optic cable network.

IYZ

Expense ratio: 0.45%

IYZ replicates the Dow Jones U.S. Select Telecommunications Index, which measures the performance of the Telecommunications sector of the U.S. equity market.

IST

Expense ratio: 0.40%

IST replicates the S&P Developed Excluding U.S. BMI Telecommunication Services Sector Index, which tracks the non-U.S. telecommunications sub-industry of developed countries.

ETF Sector, Industry, or Theme: Consumer Discretionary Equities
Companies or entities included in the ETF: Invest in companies that sell nonessential (elastic) goods and services, including retail, leisure and entertainment, media, and automotive industries.

Representative ETFs:
XLY

Expense ratio: 0.15%

XLY replicates the Consumer Discretionary Select Sector Index, which includes retail (specialty, multi-line, internet and catalog); media; hotels, restaurants, and leisure; household durables; textiles, apparel, and luxury goods; automobiles, auto components, and distributors; leisure equipment and products; and diversified consumer services.

FXD

Expense ratio: 0.70%

FXD replicates the StrataQuant Consumer Discretionary Index, an enhanced index that selects consumer discretionary stocks from the Russell 1000 Index.

VCR

Expense ratio: 0.12%

VCR replicates the MSCI US Investable Market Consumer Discretionary 25/50 Index, which consists of manufacturing and service industries that tend to be the most sensitive to economic cycles. The manufacturing industries include automotive, household durable goods, textiles and apparel, and leisure equipment. The services industries include hotels, restaurants and other leisure facilities, media production and services, and consumer retailing.

IYC

Expense ratio: 0.43%

IYC replicates the Dow Jones U.S. Consumer Services Index, which measures the performance of the consumer services sector of the U.S. equity market.

XRT

Expense ratio: 0.35%

XRT replicates the S&P Retail Select Industry Index, representing the retail sub-industry portion of the S&P TMI.

RXI

Expense ratio: 0.47%

RXI replicates the S&P Global Consumer Discretionary Index, which measures the performance of the consumer discretionary sector of global equity markets.

ETF Sector, Industry, or Theme: Consumer Staples Equities
Companies or entities included in the ETF: Invest in companies that sell essential (inelastic) goods and services, including food, beverages, tobacco, and household and personal products.

Representative ETFs:
XLP

Expense ratio: 0.15%

XLP replicates the Consumer Staples Select Sector Index, which includes companies from food and staples retailing, household products, food products, beverages, tobacco, and personal products.

VDC

Expense ratio: 0.12%

VDC replicates the MSCI US Investable Market Consumer Staples 25/50 Index, which consists of companies of various sizes whose businesses are minimally sensitive to economic cycles. It includes manufacturers and distributors of food and beverages and tobacco, nondurable household goods and personal products, food and drug retailing, and hypermarkets and consumer supercenters.

FXG

Expense ratio: 0.67%

FXG replicates the StrataQuant Consumer Staples Index, an enhanced index that selects consumer staples stocks from the Russell 1000 Index.

IYK

Expense ratio: 0.43%

IYK replicates the Dow Jones U.S. Consumer Goods Index, which measures the performance of the consumer goods sector of the U.S. equity market.

KXI

Expense ratio: 0.47%

KXI replicates the S&P Global Consumer Staples Index, which measures the performance of the consumer staples sector of global equity markets.

ETF Sector, Industry, or Theme: Emerging Markets Equities
Companies or entities included in the ETF: Invest in markets that are at the early-industrialization phase that presents high GDP growth.

Representative ETFs:
VWO

Expense ratio: 0.15%

VWO replicates the FTSE Emerging Index, which includes large and mid-cap securities from advanced and secondary emerging markets.

EEM

Expense ratio: 0.67%

EEM replicates the MSCI Emerging Markets Index, a free float-adjusted market capitalization index that measures equity market performance of emerging markets. The index consists of the following twenty-one emerging market country indices: Brazil, Chile, China, Colombia, Czech Republic, Egypt, Greece, Hungary, India, Indonesia, Korea, Malaysia, Mexico, Peru, Philippines, Poland, Russia, South Africa, Taiwan, Thailand, and Turkey.

IEMG

Expense ratio: 0.18%

IEMG replicates the MSCI Emerging Markets Investable Market Index, which is designed to measure large, mid, and small cap equity market performance in the global emerging markets.

INDA

Expense ratio: 0.68%

INDA replicates the MSCI India Index, which measures the performance of Indian equity markets.

EEMV

Expense ratio: 0.25%

EEMV replicates the MSCI Emerging Markets Minimum Volatility Index, which reflects a minimum variance strategy applied to large and mid-cap equities across twenty-one emerging market countries. The index is calculated by optimizing the MSCI Emerging Markets Index, its parent index, for the lowest absolute risk within a given set of constraints. Historically, the index has shown lower beta and volatility characteristics relative to the MSCI Emerging Markets Index.

ETF Sector, Industry, or Theme: Energy Equities
Companies or entities included in the ETF: Invest in energy producers and distributors.

Representative ETFs:
XLE

Expense ratio: 0.15%

XLE replicates the Energy Select Sector Index, including companies from the oil, gas and consumable fuels industry, as well as the energy equipment and services industry.

VDE

Expense ratio: 0.12%

VDE replicates the MSCI US Investable Market Energy 25/50 Index and consists of stocks with various sizes. These companies include the construction or provision of oil rigs, drilling equipment, and energy-related service and equipment, as well as companies engaged in the exploration, production, marketing, refining, and/or transportation of oil and gas products.

XOP

Expense ratio: 0.35%

XOP replicates the S&P Oil & Gas Exploration & Production Select Industry Index, which represents the oil and gas exploration and production sub-industry portion of the S&P Total Markets Index among the U.S. stocks.

IXC

Expense ratio: 0.47%

IXC replicates the S&P Global Energy Sector Index, which measures the performance of the energy sector of global equity markets.

IYE

Expense ratio: 0.43%

IYE replicates the Dow Jones U.S. Oil & Gas Index, which measures the performance of the energy sector of the U.S. equity market.

OIH

Expense ratio: 0.35%

OIH replicates the Market Vectors US Listed Oil Services 25 Index, which is a rules-based index intended to track the overall performance of twenty-five of the largest U.S. listed, publicly traded oil service companies.

ETF Sector, Industry, or Theme: Europe Equities
Companies or entities included in the ETF: Offer exposure to companies domiciled in Europe, including both developed and emerging markets.

Representative ETFs:
HEDJ

Expense ratio: 0.58%

HEDJ replicates the WisdomTree Europe Hedged Equity Index, which provides exposure to European equities while simultaneously neutralizing exposure to fluctuations between the Euro and the U.S. dollar.

VGK

Expense ratio: 0.12%

VGK replicates the FTSE Developed Europe Index. The FTSE Developed Europe Index is one of many indices designed to help investors benchmark their European investments. The index includes large and midcap stocks, providing coverage of the Developed markets in Europe.

EZU

Expense ratio: 0.50%

EZU replicates the MSCI EMU Index, which measures the performance of equity markets of the EMU member countries. EMU member countries are members of the European Union who have adopted the Euro as its currency.

EWG

Expense ratio: 0.48%

EWG replicates the MSCI Germany Index, which measures the performance of the German equity market.

FEZ

Expense ratio: 0.29%

FEZ replicates the EURO STOXX 50 Index, which is designed to represent the performance of some of the largest companies across components of the twenty EURO STOXX Supersector Indexes.

ETF Sector, Industry, or Theme: Financials Equities
Companies or entities included in the ETF: Invest in financial service providers, including banks, insurance, re-insurance, and financial media companies.

Representative ETFs:
XLF

Expense ratio: 0.15%

XLF replicates the Financial Select Sector Index, which includes companies from diversified financial services, insurance, commercial banks, capital markets, real estate investment trusts, thrift and mortgage finance, consumer finance, and real estate management and development.

VFH

Expense ratio: 0.12%

VFH replicates the MSCI US Investable Market Financials 25/50 Index. This consists of stocks of various sizes in the financial sector, such as banking, mortgage finance, consumer finance, specialized finance, investment banking and brokerage, asset management and custody, corporate lending, insurance, financial investment, and real estate (including REITs).

KBE

Expense ratio: 0.35%

KBE replicates the S&P Banks Select Industry Index, which consists of bank stocks.

KRE

Expense ratio: 0.35%

KRE replicates the S&P Regional Banks Select Industry Index, which consists of U.S. listed regional banks.

IYF

Expense ratio: 0.43%

IYF replicates the Dow Jones U.S. Financials Index, which measures the performance of the financial sector of the U.S. equity market.

ETF Sector, Industry, or Theme: Foreign Large Cap Equities
Companies or entities included in the ETF: Offer exposure to large capitalization companies domiciled in developed foreign countries.

Representative ETFs:
EFA

Expense ratio: 0.34%

EFA replicates the MSCI EAFE Index, which measures the performance of equity markets in European, Australasian, and Far Eastern markets.

VEA

Expense ratio: 0.09%

VEA replicates the MSCI EAFE Index, which measures the performance of equity markets in European, Australasian, and Far Eastern markets.

DBEF

Expense ratio: 0.35%

DBEF replicates the MSCI EAFE US Dollar Hedged Index, which invests in developed international stock markets while simultaneously mitigating exposure to fluctuations between the value of the U.S. dollar and non-U.S. currencies. Stocks are from Australia, Austria, Belgium, Denmark, Finland, France, Germany, Greece, Hong Kong, Ireland, Israel, Italy, Japan, Netherlands, New Zealand, Norway, Portugal, Singapore, Spain, Sweden, Switzerland, and the United Kingdom.

IEFA

Expense ratio: 0.12%

IEFA replicates the MSCI EAFE Investable Market Index, which is designed to measure large, mid, and small cap equity market performance and includes stocks from Europe, Australasia, and the Far East.

EFAV

Expense ratio: 0.20%

EFAV replicates the MSCI EAFE Minimum Volatility Index, reflecting a minimum variance strategy relative to the large and mid-cap equity universe across twenty-two Developed Markets countries, excluding the U.S. and Canada. Historically, the index has shown lower beta and volatility characteristics relative to the MSCI EAFE Index.

SCHF

Expense ratio: 0.08%

SCHF replicates the FTSE Developed excluding U.S. Index. The FTSE Developed ex-US Index is comprised of approximately 85% large-cap stocks and 15% mid-cap stocks from more than twenty developed international markets, excluding the US.

HEFA

Expense ratio: 0.35%

HEFA replicates the MSCI EAFE 100% Hedged to USD Index, which seeks to track the investment results of an index composed of large- and mid-capitalization equities in Europe, Australasia, and the Far East. The results are tracked while simultaneously mitigating exposure to fluctuations between the value of the component currencies and the value of the U.S. dollar.

EFV

Expense ratio: 0.40%

EFV replicates the MSCI EAFE Value Index, which measures the performance of stocks in European, Australasian, and Far Eastern markets that represent value characteristics.

IDV

Expense ratio: 0.50%

IDV replicates the Dow Jones EPAC Select Dividend Index, which measures the performance of a select group of companies that have consistently provided relatively high dividend yields over a substantial amount of time.

ETF Sector, Industry, or Theme: Foreign Small & Mid Cap Equities
Companies or entities included in the ETF: Offer exposure to small and mid-capitalization companies domiciled in developed foreign countries.

Representative ETFs:
SCZ

Expense ratio: 0.40%

SCZ replicates the MSCI EAFE Small Cap Index, which measures the performance of small cap stocks in European, Australasian, and Far Eastern markets.

VSS

Expense ratio: 0.19%

VSS replicates the FTSE Global Small Cap excluding US Index, which includes approximately 3,300 stocks of companies in more than 46 countries from both developed and emerging markets around the world.

DLS

Expense ratio: 0.58%

DLS replicates the WisdomTree International Small Cap Dividend Index, which measures the performance of the small-capitalization segment of the dividend-paying market in the industrialized world outside the U.S. and Canada.

SCHC

Expense ratio: 0.19%

SCHC replicates the FTSE Developed Small Cap excluding U.S. Liquid Index. The FTSE Developed Small Cap ex-US Liquid Index is comprised of small-cap companies in developed countries, excluding the United States. The index defines the small-cap universe as approximately the bottom 10% of the eligible universe with a minimum free float capitalization of $150 million.

GWX

Expense ratio: 0.40%

GWX replicates the S&P Developed excluding U.S. Under USD 2 Billion Index, representing publicly traded companies from developed countries outside of the United States.

FNDC

Expense ratio: 0.48%

FNDC replicates the Russell Fundamental Developed excluding U.S. Small Company Index, which is designed to provide exposure to international small companies using the fundamental index methodology.

DIM

Expense ratio: 0.58%

DIM replicates the WisdomTree International Mid Cap Dividend Index, measuring the performance of the mid-capitalization segment of the dividend-paying market in the industrialized world outside of the United States and Canada.

ETF Sector, Industry, or Theme: Global Equities
Companies or entities included in the ETF: Offer investors exposure to equities from all around the world, from both developed and emerging markets.

Representative ETFs:
VEU

Expense ratio: 0.15%

VEU replicates the FTSE All-World excluding US Index, which includes approximately 2,200 stocks of companies in 46 countries, from both developed and emerging markets around the world.

ACWI

Expense ratio: 0.33%

ACWI replicates the MSCI All Country World Index, which is designed to measure the performance of global equity markets.

VT

Expense ratio: 0.18%

VT replicates the FTSE Global All Cap Index, which includes approximately 7,400 stocks of companies located in 47 countries, including both developed and emerging markets.

VXUS

Expense ratio: 0.14%

VXUS replicates the MSCI All Country World excluding USA Investable Market Index, which measures the investment return of stocks issued by companies located outside of the United States.

ACWX

Expense ratio: 0.33%

ACWX replicates the MSCI All Country World excluding U.S. Index. This index measures the performance of global equity markets, excluding the United States.

ACWV

Expense ratio: 0.20%

ACWV replicates the MSCI All Country World Minimum Volatility Index, reflecting a minimum variance strategy applied to large and mid-cap equities across 45 developed and emerging market countries. Historically, the index has shown lower beta and volatility characteristics relative to the MSCI ACWI Index.

IXUS

Expense ratio: 0.14%

IXUS replicates the MSCI ACWI excluding USA Investable Market Index, which measures the combined equity market performance of developed and emerging market countries, excluding the United States.

IOO

Expense ratio: 0.40%

IOO replicates the S&P Global 100 Index, which is designed to measure the performance of 100 large transitional companies that are of major importance in global markets.

ETF Sector, Industry, or Theme: Health & Biotech Equities
Companies or entities included in the ETF: Invest in companies involved in the healthcare and biotechnology industries, including healthcare providers, services, medical devices, and pharmaceuticals.

Representative ETFs:

XLV

Expense ratio: 0.15%

XLV replicates the Health Care Select Sector Index, including pharmaceuticals, health care providers and services, health care equipment and supplies, biotechnology, life sciences tools and services, and health care technology.

IBB

Expense ratio: 0.48%

IBB replicates the NASDAQ Biotechnology Index, including companies that are classified as either biotechnology or pharmaceutical.

VHT

Expense ratio: 0.12%

VHT replicates the MSCI US Investable Market Health Care 25/50 Index, which consists of stocks of various sizes and is made up of two main industry groups: manufacturers of health care equipment and supplies and those that provide health care related services, or those that do research, development, production, and marketing of pharmaceuticals and biotechnology products.

FXH

Expense ratio: 0.66%

FXH replicates the StrataQuant Health Care Index, an enhanced index that selects health care stocks from the Russell 1000 Index.

IYH

Expense ratio: 0.43%

IYH replicates the Dow Jones U.S. Health Care Index, which measures the performance of the healthcare sector of the U.S. equity market.

XBI

Expense ratio: 0.35%

XBI replicates the S&P Biotechnology Select Industry Index and represents the biotechnology sub-industry portion of the S&P Total Markets Index (S&P TMI) in the U.S. market.

IXJ

Expense ratio: 0.47%

IXJ replicates the S&P Global Healthcare Sector Index, which includes healthcare providers, biotechnology companies, and manufacturers of advanced medical devices and pharmaceuticals.

PJP

Expense ratio: 0.58%

PJP replicates the Dynamic Pharmaceuticals Intellidex Index, which is comprised of stocks of U.S. pharmaceutical companies. The Index is designed to provide capital appreciation by thoroughly evaluating companies based on a variety of investment merit criteria.

ETF Sector, Industry, or Theme: Industrials Equities
Companies or entities included in the ETF: Invest in companies in the industrials industry, including both U.S. and international stocks, as well as aerospace and defense companies.

Representative ETFs:
XLI

Expense ratio: 0.15%

XLI replicates the Industrial Select Sector Index and includes industrial conglomerates, aerospace and defense, machinery, air freight and logistics, road and rail, commercial services and supplies, electrical equipment, construction and engineering, building products, airlines, and trading companies and distributors.

VIS

Expense ratio: 0.12%

VIS replicates the MSCI US Investable Market Industrials 25/50 Index and consists of stocks of various sizes, including the manufacture and distribution of capital goods, the provision of commercial services and supplies, and the provision of transportation services.

ITA

Expense ratio: 0.43%

ITA replicates the Dow Jones U.S. Select Aerospace & Defense Index, which measures the performance of the aerospace and defense sector of the U.S. equity market.

IYJ

Expense ratio: 0.43%

IYJ replicates the Dow Jones U.S. Industrials Index, which measures the performance of the industrial sector of the U.S. equity market.

ETF Sector, Industry, or Theme: Japan Equities
Companies or entities included in the ETF: Invest in companies domiciled in Japan.

Representative ETF:
EWJ

Expense ratio: 0.48%

EWJ replicates the MSCI Japan Index, which measures the performance of the Japanese equity market.

DXJ

Expense ratio: 0.48%

DXJ replicates the WisdomTree Japan Hedged Equity Index, which is designed to provide exposure to equity securities in Japan while simultaneously hedging exposure to fluctuations between the value of the U.S. dollar and the Japanese yen.

DBJP

Expense ratio: 0.45%

DBJP replicates the MSCI Japan US Dollar Hedged Index, which is designed to provide exposure to Japanese equity markets while simultaneously mitigating exposure to fluctuations between the value of the U.S. dollar and Japanese yen.

HEWJ

Expense ratio: 0.48%

HEWJ replicates the MSCI Japan 100% Hedged to USD Index, which seeks to track the investment results of an index composed of large- and mid-capitalization Japanese equities while mitigating exposure to currency risk.

DFJ

Expense ratio: 0.58%

DFJ replicates the WisdomTree Japan Small Cap Dividend Index, which measures the performance of dividend-paying small capitalization companies in Japan.

ETF Sector, Industry, or Theme: Large Cap Blend Equities
Companies or entities included in the ETF: Invest in large cap stocks in the U.S. that are mixes of growth and value.

Representative ETFs:
SPY

Expense ratio: 0.09%

SPY replicates the S&P 500 Index, which measures the performance of the large capitalization sector of the U.S. equity market. SPY is considered one of the best representations of the domestic economy.

IVV

Expense ratio: 0.07%

IVV replicates the S&P 500 Index, which measures the performance of the large capitalization sector of the U.S. equity market. IVV is considered one of the best representations of the domestic economy.

VOO

Expense ratio: 0.05%

VOO replicates the S&P 500 Index, which measures the performance of the large capitalization sector of the U.S. equity market. VOO is considered one of the best representations of the domestic economy.

IWB

Expense ratio: 0.15%

IWB replicates the Russell 1000 Index, which is capitalization-weighted and consists of the 1,000 largest companies domiciled in the U.S. and its territories.

RSP

Expense ratio: 0.40%

RSP replicates the S&P Equal Weight Index. The S&P Equal Weight Index is based on the S&P 500. The S&P EWI measures the performance of the same 500 companies; sector weights in the S&P EWI will differ.

VV

Expense ratio: 0.09%

VV replicates the CRSP US Large Cap Index, which is a broadly diversified index of stocks of predominantly large U.S. companies.

SPLV

Expense ratio: 0.25%

SPLV replicates the S&P 500 Low Volatility Index, which consists of the 100 stocks from the S&P 500 Index with the lowest realized volatility over the past twelve months.

OEF

Expense ratio: 0.20%

OEF replicates the S&P 100 Index, which measures the performance of stocks from a broad range of industries chosen for market size, liquidity, and industry group representation.

ETF Sector, Industry, or Theme: Large Cap Growth Equities
Companies or entities included in the ETF: Invest in large cap stocks in the U.S. that are low-dividend paying.

Representative ETFs:
QQQ

Expense ratio: 0.20%
QQQ replicates the NASDAQ-100 Index, which includes 100 of the largest domestic and international nonfinancial companies listed on the Nasdaq Stock Market based on market capitalization. The index focuses most heavily on companies in the technology sector.

IWF

Expense ratio: 0.20%
IWF replicates the Russell 1000 Growth Index, which measures the performance of the large capitalization growth sector of the U.S. equity market.

VUG

Expense ratio: 0.09%
VUG replicates the MSCI US Prime Market Growth Index, which is a broadly diversified index of growth stocks of predominantly large U.S. companies.

IVW

Expense ratio: 0.18%
IVW replicates the S&P 500/Citigroup Growth Index, which measures the performance of the large capitalization growth sector of the U.S. equity market.

SCHG

Expense ratio: 0.07%
SCHG replicates the Dow Jones U.S. Large-Cap Growth Total Stock Market Total Return Index. It includes the largest 750 stocks that demonstrate growth style characteristics.

MGK

Expense ratio: 0.11%
MGK replicates the MSCI US Large Cap Growth Index, which represents the growth companies of the MSCI US Large Cap 300 Index.

RPG

Expense ratio: 0.35%
RPG replicates the S&P 500/Citigroup Pure Growth Index. It is narrow in focus, containing only those S&P 500 companies with strong growth characteristics as selected by S&P.

ETF Sector, Industry, or Theme: Large Cap Value Equities
Companies or entities included in the ETF: Invest in large cap stocks in the U.S. that are high-dividend paying.

Representative ETFs:
IWD
Expense ratio: 0.21%

IWD replicates the Russell 1000 Value Index, which measures the performance of the large capitalization value sector of the U.S. equity market.

VIG
Expense ratio: 0.10%

VIG replicates the NASDAQ US Dividend Achievers Select Index, which tracks stocks that have a history of increasing dividends for at least ten consecutive years. The fund will hold all the stocks in the index in approximately the same proportions as their weightings in the index.

VTV
Expense ratio: 0.09%

VTV replicates the MSCI US Prime Market Value Index, which represents the universe of predominantly large-capitalization companies in the U.S. equity market.

DVY
Expense ratio: 0.40%

DVY replicates the Dow Jones U.S. Select Dividend Index, which screens stocks by dividend per share growth rate, dividend payout percentage rate, and average daily dollar trading volume. Stocks are selected based on dividend yield.

SDY
Expense ratio: 0.35%

SDY replicates the S&P High Yield Dividend Aristocrats Index. It is comprised of the fifty highest dividend yielding constituents for at least twenty-five consecutive years. These stocks have both capital growth and dividend income characteristics, as opposed to stocks that are pure yield or pure capital-oriented.

VYM
Expense ratio: 0.10%

VYM replicates the FTSE High Dividend Yield Index and includes stocks with the highest dividend yields, excluding REITs.
DIA
Expense ratio: 0.17%

DIA replicates the Dow Jones Industrial Average. The Dow Jones Industrial Average is a price-weighted index of 30 "blue-chip" U.S. stocks.

IVE

Expense ratio: 0.18%

IVE replicates the S&P 500 Value Index, which measures the performance of the large-capitalization value sector of the U.S. equity market.

ETF Sector, Industry, or Theme: Mid Cap Blend Equities
Companies or entities included in the ETF: Invest in mid cap stocks in the U.S. that are a mixture of growth and value.

Representative ETFs:
IJH

Expense ratio: 0.15%

IJH replicates the S&P MidCap 400 Index, which measures the performance of the mid-capitalization sector of the U.S. equity market.

MDY

Expense ratio: 0.25%

MDY replicates the S&P MidCap 400 Index, which measures the performance of the mid-capitalization sector of the U.S. equity market.

VO

Expense ratio: 0.09%

VO replicates the CRSP US Mid Cap Index. The MSCI US Mid Cap 450 Index represents the universe of mid-capitalization companies in the U.S. equity market.

IWR

Expense ratio: 0.22%

IWR replicates the Russell Midcap Index, which measures the performance of the mid-capitalization sector of the U.S. equity market.

ETF Sector, Industry, or Theme: Mid Cap Growth Equities
Companies or entities included in the ETF: Invest in mid cap stocks in the U.S. that are low-dividend paying.

Representative ETFs:
IWP

Expense ratio: 0.25%

IWP replicates the Russell Midcap Growth Index, which measures the performance of the mid-capitalization growth sector of the U.S. equity market.

IJK

Expense ratio: 0.25%

IJK replicates the S&P MidCap 400/Citigroup Growth Index, which measures the performance of the mid-capitalization growth sector of the U.S. equity market.

VOT
Expense ratio: 0.09%

VOT replicates the MSCI US Mid Cap Growth Index and represents the growth companies of the MSCI U.S. Mid Cap 450 Index.

ETF Sector, Industry, or Theme: Mid Cap Value Equities
Companies or entities included in the ETF: Invest in small cap stocks in the U.S. that are high-dividend paying.

Representative ETFs:
IWS
Expense ratio: 0.25%

IWS replicates the Russell Midcap Value Index, which measures the performance of the mid-capitalization value sector of the U.S. equity market.

VOE
Expense ratio: 0.09%

VOE replicates the CRSP US Mid Cap Value Index, representing the value companies of the CRSP U.S. Mid Cap Index.

IJJ
Expense ratio: 0.27%

IJJ replicates the S&P MidCap 400/Citigroup Value Index, which measures the   performance of the mid-capitalization value sector of the U.S. equity market.

DON
Expense ratio: 0.38%

DON replicates the WisdomTree MidCap Dividend Index, which measures the performance of the mid-capitalization segment of the US dividend-paying market.

ETF Sector, Industry, or Theme: Small Cap Blend Equities
Companies or entities included in the ETF: Invest in small cap stocks in the U.S. that are mixes of growth and value.

Representative ETFs:
IWM
Expense ratio: 0.20%

IWM replicates the Russell 2000 Index, which measures the performance of the small-cap segment of the U.S. equity universe and is comprised of the smallest 2,000 companies in the Russell 3000.

IJR

Expense ratio: 0.17%

IJR replicates the S&P SmallCap 600 Index, which measures the performance of the small capitalization sector of the U.S. equity market.

VB

Expense ratio: 0.09%

VB replicates the CRSP US Small Cap Index, which represents the universe of small-capitalization companies in the U.S. equity market.

SCHA

Expense ratio: 0.08%

SCHA replicates the Dow Jones U.S. Small-Cap Total Stock Market Total Return Index, representing the stocks ranked 751 to 2,500 by full market capitalization. This calculation is float-adjusted and market cap weighted.

PRFZ

Expense ratio: 0.39%

PRFZ replicates the FTSE RAFI US 1500 Small-Mid Index, tracking the performance of small and medium-sized U.S. companies.

IWC

Expense ratio: 0.60%

IWC replicates the Russell Microcap Index, which measures the performance of the microcap sector of the U.S. equity market.

VTWO

Expense ratio: 0.15%

VTWO replicates the Russell 2000 Index. It includes approximately 2,000 of the smallest securities based on a combination of their market cap and current index membership.

ETF Sector, Industry, or Theme: Small Cap Growth Equities
Companies or entities included in the ETF: Invest in small cap stocks in the U.S. that are low-dividend paying.

Representative ETFs:
IWO

Expense ratio: 0.25%

IWO replicates the Russell 2000 Growth Index, which measures the performance of the small capitalization growth sector of the U.S. equity market.

VBK

Expense ratio: 0.09%

VBK replicates the MSCI US Small Cap Growth Index, which represents the growth companies of the MSCI US Small Cap 1750 Index.

IJT

Expense ratio: 0.25%

IJT replicates the S&P SmallCap 600/Citigroup Growth Index, which measures the performance of the small capitalization growth sector of the U.S. equity market.

SLYG

Expense ratio: 0.15%

SLYG replicates the S&P SmallCap 600 Growth Index, which consists of growth stocks in the S&P SmallCap 600 Index.

RZG

Expense ratio: 0.35%

RZG replicates the S&P SmallCap 600/Citigroup Pure Growth Index. It is narrow in focus, containing only those S&P SmallCap 600 companies with strong growth characteristics as selected by S&P.

VTWG

Expense ratio: 0.20%

VTWG replicates the Russell 2000 Growth Index, which measures the performance of the small capitalization growth sector of the U.S. equity market.

ETF Sector, Industry, or Theme: Small Cap Value Equities
Companies or entities included in the ETF: Invest in small cap stocks in the U.S. that are high-dividend paying.

Representative ETF:
VBR

Expense ratio: 0.09%

VBR replicates the MSCI US Small Cap Value Index. The MSCI US Small Cap Value Index represents the value companies of the MSCI US Small Cap 1750 Index.

IWN

Expense ratio: 0.25%

IWN replicates the Russell 2000 Value Index, which measures the performance of the small capitalization value sector of the U.S. equity market.

IJS

Expense ratio: 0.25%

IJS replicates the S&P SmallCap 600/Citigroup Value Index, which measures the performance of the small capitalization value sector of the U.S. equity market.

DES

Expense ratio: 0.38%

DES replicates the WisdomTree SmallCap Dividend Index, measuring the performance of the small-capitalization segment of the US dividend-paying market.

ETF Sector, Industry, or Theme: Latin America Equities
Companies or entities included in the ETF: Invest in companies domiciled primarily in Brazil, Mexico, Peru, and Chili.

Representative ETFs:
EWZ

Expense ratio: 0.62%

EWZ replicates the MSCI Brazil 25/50 Index, which is designed to measure broad-based equity market performance in Brazil.

EWW

Expense ratio: 0.49%

EWW replicates the MSCI Mexico IMI 25/50 Index, measuring broad-based equity market performance in Mexico.

ILF

Expense ratio: 0.49%

ILF replicates the S&P Latin America 40 Index, which measures the performance of four Latin American equity markets: Mexico, Brazil, Argentina, and Chile.

ECH

Expense ratio: 0.62%

ECH replicates the MSCI Chile Investable Market Index, which measures the performance of the Chilean equity market.

EPU

Expense ratio: 0.62%

EPU replicates the MSCI All Peru Capped Index, which measures the performance of the Peruvian equity market.

ETF Sector, Industry, or Theme: MLPs
Companies or entities included in the ETF: Invest in Master Limited Partnerships (MLPs). These companies are generally involved in the exploration, production, or transportation of energies such as oil and natural gas.

Representative ETFs:
AMLP

Expense ratio: 5.43%
AMLP replicates the Alerian MLP Infrastructure Index, which is designed to give investors exposure to the infrastructure component of the Master Limited Partnership asset class.

AMJ

Expense ratio: 0.85%
AMJ replicates the Alerian MLP Index, which currently operates in the energy infrastructure industry. This sector owns assets such as pipelines that transport crude oil, natural gas, and other refined petroleum products.

MLPI

Expense ratio: 0.85%
AMJ replicates the Alerian MLP Index, which currently operates in the energy infrastructure industry. This sector owns assets such as pipelines that transport crude oil, natural gas, and other refined petroleum products. Constituents each   earn at least 50% of EBITDA from assets that are not directly exposed to changes in commodity prices.

ETF Sector, Industry, or Theme: Materials Equities
Companies or entities included in the ETF: Invest in companies that produce basic materials.

Representative ETFs:
VAW

Expense ratio: 0.12%
VAW replicates MSCI US Investable Market Materials 25/50 Index, and consists of stocks of various sizes. This sector is made up of companies in a wide range of commodity-related manufacturing industries.

XLB

Expense ratio: 0.15%
XLB replicates the Materials Select Sector Index, including the following industries: chemicals, metals and mining, paper and forest products, containers and packaging, and construction materials.

IYM

Expense ratio: 0.43%

IYM replicates the Dow Jones U.S. Basic Materials Index, which measures the performance of the basic materials sector of the U.S. equity market.

MXI

Expense ratio: 0.47%

MXI replicates the S&P Global Materials Index, which measures the performance of the materials sector of global equity markets.

ETF Sector, Industry, or Theme: Technology Equities
Companies or entities included in the ETF: Invest in companies that produce high-tech related products, excluding the IT industry.

Representative ETFs:
XLK

Expense ratio: 0.15%

XLK replicates the Technology Select Sector Index, including computers and peripherals, software, diversified telecommunication services, communications equipment, semiconductor and equipment, Internet software and services, IT services, wireless telecommunication services, electronic equipment and instruments, and office electronics.

VGT

Expense ratio: 0.14%

VGT replicates the MSCI US Investable Market Information Technology 25/50 Index, including stocks of various sizes.

FDN

Expense ratio: 0.57%
FDN replicates the Dow Jones Internet Index.

IYW

Expense ratio: 0.43%

IYW replicates the Dow Jones U.S. Technology Index, which measures the performance of the technology sector of the U.S. equity market.

IGM

Expense ratio: 0.47%

IGM replicates the S&P North American Technology Sector Index, which measures the performance of the technology sector of the U.S. equity market.

IGV

Expense ratio: 0.47%

IGV replicates the S&P North American Technology-Software Index, which measures the performance of U.S.-traded software-related stocks.

IXN

Expense ratio: 0.47%

IXN replicates the S&P Global Information Technology Sector Index, which measures the performance of the technology sector of the global equity market.

ETF Sector, Industry, or Theme: Transportation Equities
Companies or entities included in the ETF: Invest in companies that produce transportation products and provide transportation services.

Representative ETFs:
IYT

Expense ratio: 0.43%

IYT replicates the Dow Jones Transportation Average Index, which measures the performance of the transportation sector of the U.S. equity market.

XTN

Expense ratio: 0.35%

XTN replicates the S&P Transportation Select Industry Index, which represents the transportation sub-industry portion of the S&P Total Stock Market Index.

SEA

Expense ratio: 0.66%

SEA replicates the Dow Jones Global Shipping Index, which measures the stock performance of high dividend-paying companies in the global shipping industry.

ETF Sector, Industry, or Theme: Utilities Equities
Companies or entities included in the ETF: Invest in companies that provide utility services.

Representative ETFs:
XLU

Expense ratio: 0.15%

XLU replicates the Utilities Select Sector Index, including electric utilities, multi- utilities, independent power producers and energy traders, and gas utilities.

VPU

Expense ratio: 0.12%

VPU replicates the MSCI US Investable Market Utilities 25/50 Index. It consists of various sizes of stock, including companies regarding electric, gas, or water utilities, as well as companies that operate as independent producers and/or distributors of power, including both nuclear and nonnuclear facilities.

FXU

Expense ratio: 0.70%

FXU replicates the StrataQuant Utilities Index, an enhanced index, selecting utilities stocks from the Russell 1000 Index.

IGF

Expense ratio: 0.47%

IGF replicates the S&P Global Infrastructure Index, which measures the performance of the global infrastructure sector.

IDU

Expense ratio: 0.43%

IDU replicates the Dow Jones U.S. Utilities Index, which measures the performance of the utilities sector of the U.S. equity market.

ETF Sector, Industry, or Theme: Volatility Hedged Equities
Companies or entities included in the ETF: Invest in equities, as well as volatility derivatives. By investing partially in volatility, these ETFs offer a downside hedge for their equity exposure.

Representative ETFs:
PHDG

Expense ratio: 0.40%

PHDG replicates the S&P 500 Dynamic VEQTOR Total Return Index, providing investors with broad equity market exposure with an implied volatility hedge by dynamically allocating its notional investments among three components: equity, volatility, and cash.

VQT

Expense ratio: 0.95%

VQT replicates the S&P 500 Dynamic VEQTOR Total Return Index, providing investors with broad equity market exposure with an implied volatility hedge by dynamically allocating its notional investments among three components: equity, volatility and cash.

ETF Sector, Industry, or Theme: Water Equities
Companies or entities included in the ETF: Invest in companies that

produce water services.

Representative ETFs:
PHO

Expense ratio: 0.61%

PHO replicates the NASDAQ OMX US Water Index, tracking the performance of U.S. exchange-listed companies that create products designed to conserve and purify water for homes, businesses, and industries.

CGW

Expense ratio: 0.65%

CGW replicates the S&P Global Water Index, which is comprised of approximately 50 securities that are selected based on the relative importance of the global water industry.

PIO

Expense ratio: 0.76%

PIO replicates the NASDAQ OMX Global Water Index, which is designed to invest in companies listed on a global exchange that create products designed to conserve and purify water for homes, businesses and industries.

ETF Sector, Industry, or Theme: Inverse Equities
Companies or entities included in the ETF: ETFs that are profitable for an investor during a market decline.

Representative ETFs:
SH

Expense ratio: 0.89%

SH is a leveraged ETF that seeks daily investment results that correspond to the inverse of the daily performance of the S&P 500 Index.

SDS

Expense ratio: 0.89%

SDS is a leveraged ETF that seeks daily investment results that correspond to the doubling inverse of the daily performance of the S&P 500 Index.

SPXS

Expense ratio: 0.95%

SPXS is a leveraged ETF that seeks daily investment results that correspond to the trebling inverse of the daily performance of the S&P 500 Index.

VXX

Expense ratio: 0.89%

VXX replicates the S&P 500 VIX Short-Term Futures Index Total Return. It is a proxy of market panic and decreases when the market volatility or panic is low.

ETF Sector, Industry, or Theme: Leveraged Equities

Companies or entities included in the ETF: ETFs that boost returns on an index by using financial derivatives and debt.

Representative ETFs:

SSO

Expense ratio: 0.89%

SSO is a leveraged ETF. This index seeks daily investment results that correspond to twice (200%) the daily performance of the S&P 500 Index.

TQQQ

Expense ratio: 0.95%

TQQQ is a leveraged ETF. The Index includes 100 of the largest domestic and international nonfinancial companies listed on the Nasdaq Stock Market based on market capitalization.

FAS

Expense ratio: 0.95%

FAS is a leveraged ETF. The Russell 1000 Financial Services Index is a capitalization-weighted index of companies that provide financial services.

UPRO

Expense ratio: 0.95%

UPRO is a leveraged ETF. The index measures the performance of large cap U.S. equities.

QLD

Expense ratio: 0.95%

QLD is a leveraged ETF. ProShares Ultra QQQ seeks daily investment results that correspond to twice (200%) the daily performance of the NASDAQ-100 Index.

TNA

Expense ratio: 0.95%

TNA is a leveraged ETF tracking the Russell 2000 Index, which measures the performance of the small-cap segment of the U.S. equity universe. It is comprised of the 2,000 smallest companies in the Russell 3000 Index, representing approximately 10% of the total market capitalization of that Index.

SPXL

Expense ratio: 0.95%

SPXL is a leveraged ETF that is linked to Direxion. The index measures the performance of large cap U.S. equities.

ETF Sector, Industry, or Theme: Global Real Estate Equities
Companies or entities included in the ETF: Invest in real estate companies from all over the world.

Representative ETFs:
RWX

Expense ratio: 0.59%

RWX replicates the Dow Jones Global ex-U.S. Real Estate Securities Index, which measures the performance of publicly traded real estate securities in developed and emerging countries, excluding the United States.

VNQI

Expense ratio: 0.24%

VNQI replicates the S&P Global ex-U.S. Property Index, which includes real estate investment trusts (REITs) and real estate operating companies (REOCs) in emerging markets and developed markets outside of the United States.

RWO

Expense ratio: 0.50%

RWO replicates the Dow Jones Global Select Real Estate Securities Index, which measures the performance of publicly traded real estate securities in developed and emerging countries.

ETF Sector, Industry, or Theme: Real Estate Equities
Companies or entities included in the ETF: Invest in the U.S. real estate market, primarily Real Estate Investment Trusts (REITs).

Representative ETFs:
VNQ

Expense ratio: 0.12%

VNQ replicates the MSCI US REIT Index, which is designed to cover about two-thirds of the value of the entire U.S. REIT market.

IYR

Expense ratio: 0.43%

IYR replicates the Dow Jones U.S. Real Estate Index, which measures the performance of the real estate industry of the U.S. equity market.

ICF

Expense ratio: 0.35%

ICF replicates the Cohen & Steers Realty Majors Index, which consists of selected real estate investment trusts (REITs).

RWR

Expense ratio: 0.25%

RWR replicates the Dow Jones U.S. Select REIT Index. The Dow Jones U.S. Select REIT index is comprised of companies whose charters are the equity ownership and operation of commercial real estate.

3 INVESTMENT UNIVERSE: AVAILABLE INSTRUMENTS

Baroque Omaha: Can you tell us about different financial assets in the market? What kind of asset in the market can we invest in, and why should I invest on my own?

Professor Dong: Roughly speaking, there are four categories of financial instruments in the United States: equity, bond, derivatives, and alternatives. However, not all of these assets are the ones that individual investors might have access to. This access limit is greatly relieved by the creation of various types of ETFs.

Equity	1. Common stocks	A share of publicly traded ownership of the firm. Benefits from the firm's profit after the firm's debt is paid off. Responsible for loss if the firm fails to generate profit.
	2. Preferred stocks	Similar to common stocks, but receive higher and more stable dividends. Dividends have higher priority compared to common share benefit distribution. Not eligible to vote on firm decisions.
	3. Private equities	Similar to common stocks. Publicly traded shares are called stock; privately held shares do not have a particular name but simply private equity.
	4. REITs	Real estate investment trust. A convenient way to expend minimal cost and gain access to

		a basket of managed property or the mortgage interest rate market.
	ETFs of 1-4.	Various ETFs that invest in the equities mentioned above. The ETF basket can be stock indexes, which are equities classified by industry, country, risk profile, stock size, dividend profile, etc.
	6. Checking account	Bank savings account linked to check books.
	7. Savings (money market) account	Bank savings account that can be deposited and withdrawn without restriction.
	8. Certificate of Deposit (CD)	Fixed-term savings account. Early withdrawals incur penalty.
Bond	9. Treasury bond	Bond issued by the U.S. Department of Treasury. Short term bills are regarded as nearly risk-free.
	10. State and Local Government Bond	Some of these bonds are called municipal bonds and are tax-exempt for local residents. Bond cash flow can be backed by tax revenue or project return, which initiates the issuing of the bond.
	11. Semi-government Bond	So called (semi-)agency bonds, whose issuers are (semi-) guaranteed and backed by the government, such as Fanni Mae, Freddie Mac, Sallie Mae, etc.
	12. Corporate Bond	Borrowings from the firms and payoff are from the firms' future revenue or future issuance of new debt.
	13. Asset-backed Securities	Pooled assets that generate revenue to pay off a debt obligation. The assets can be various types of debts that produce cash flows, such as auto loan, home mortgage, etc.

	ETFs of 6-13.	Various ETFs that invest in the fixed-income instruments mentioned above. The ETF basket can be made up of bond indexes, which are bonds classified by industry, country, credit rating, coupon level, seniority, etc.
Derivatives	15. Options	Call and put options that grant privilege – *but no* obligation – to purchase or sell assets at a pre-determined price.
	16. Futures	Contracts that grant privilege *and* obligation to purchase or sell assets at a pre-determined price.
	17. Forwards	Similar to futures, but the contract is not standardized. It is not exchange traded with central clearing house or daily settlement.
	18. Swaps	Similar to a series of forward contracts that transaction parties use to exchange cash flows multiple times in the future.
	19. Collatera-lized Debt Obligations	A structured financial product that pools cash flow-generating assets and repackages this asset pool into tranches with different repayment schedule to sell to investors.
	20. Fund of funds	A fund that purchases other funds and optimizes the funds combination. Helps investors gain access to high-entry barrier hedge funds or foreign funds.
	21. Hedge funds	Funds that use multiple and sometimes more aggressive strategies to pursue higher returns. The name can be misleading as some hedge funds do not employ hedging actions.
	ETF of 15-21.	Various ETFs that invest in the derivative instruments mentioned above.
Alternatives	23. Insurance	Life, property, and investment purpose-combined downside protection.
	24. Foreign Exchange	The largest financial market. Pursues highly leveraged profit from change of exchange rates.
	25.	Buying property, and pursuing land and

	Real Estate (single property)	property feature appreciation.
	26. Collections	Buying and holding collections, and pursue single-asset appreciation.
	27. Venture Capital	Investments on start-up companies that plan to foster the future share appreciation and firm profits.
	28. Leveraged Buyout	Investments on matured companies that make public companies private, as well as gain capital appreciation.
	ETF of the 23-28.	Various ETFs that invest in the alternative instruments mentioned above.

Moselle Omaha: What are the advantages of investing in equity?

Professor Dong: Let's first specify what equity means in this book. Equity includes all of the major types of assets traded in New York Security Exchange (NYSE) or NASDAQ. Specifically, equity in this book means asset common stocks, preferred stock ETFs, other equity-based ETFs, REITs, and close-ended funds.

Equity	1. Common stocks	Considerable returns. Risk level varies from low to high but can usually be hedged. High liquidity. High transparency.
	2. Preferred stocks	Not directly accessible by individual investors but can be purchased via preferred stock ETFs. Returns are stable and risk is low. High transparency.
	3. Private equities	High return and high risk. Not accessible by individual investors. Low liquidity. Low transparency.
	4. REITs	Return and risk vary. REIT ETF risk can usually be hedged. High transparency.
	ETFs of 1-4.	ETFs are in general liquid. Risk-hedging tools are widely available for these ETFs.
Bond	6.	Very low risk. Negative return if considering

	Checking account	the time value of money. High transparency.
	7. Savings (money market) account	Very low risk. Negative return when account fee presents. High transparency.
	8. Certificate of Deposit (CD)	Very low risk. Low return with an early withdrawal penalty. High transparency.
	9. Treasury bond	Low return with a low-to-medium level risk. High transparency.
	10. State and Local Government Bond	Low return. Risk level varies. Low to high transparency.
	11. Semi-government Bond	Low return. Risk level varies. Low transparency.
	12. Corporate Bond	Low-to-medium return. Risk level varies. Low liquidity. Low to high transparency.
	13. Asset-backed Securities	Return and risk vary. Low transparency.
	ETFs of 6-13.	ETFs are generally not liquid. Transaction cost and expense ratio are high. High transparency.
Derivatives	15. Options	High return and high risk. Requires vigorous mathematical analysis. High transparency.
	16. Futures	High return and high risk. Requires highly skillful trading and specific sector understanding. High transparency.

	17. Forwards	High return and high risk. Requires highly skillful trading and specific sector understanding. Low transparency.
	18. Swaps	High return and high risk. Requires vigorous mathematical analysis. Not accessible by individual traders. Low transparency.
	19. Collatera-lized Debt Obligations	High return and high risk. Requires vigorous mathematical analysis. Not accessible by individual traders. Low transparency.
	20. Fund of funds	Very high transaction costs and expense ratios. Return and risk vary. Low transparency.
	21. Hedge funds	Very high transaction costs and expense ratios. High return and risk. Restricted asset entry and withdrawal. High entry barrier. Low transparency.
	ETF of 15-21.	ETFs on derivatives are not very liquid.
Alternatives	23. Insurance	Not mainly for investment purposes. Intended to hedge downside risk. The return is not as high as equity. Low transparency.
	24. Foreign Exchange	High return and high risk. Requires highly skillful trading. High transparency.
	25. Real Estate (single property)	Return varies. Risk is high. Not liquid and high transaction cost. Low transparency.
	26. Collections	High return and high risk. Requires sophisticated knowledge. Low transparency.
	27. Venture Capital	High return and high risk. Requires sophisticated knowledge. Not accessible to individual investors. Low transparency.
	28. Leveraged Buyout	High return and high risk. Requires sophisticated knowledge. Not accessible to individual investors. Low transparency.

ETF of the   Few ETFs.
23-28.

Wanna Buffet: Should I invest in equity then? Does it work for everyone?

Professor Dong: Public equity, which is usually regarded as including common stock and preferred stock, works for many different types of investors. This asset class generally generates high return and has reasonable risk. The risk can usually be hedged by available derivatives or inverse ETFs, which are swap-based.

Compared to other asset classes that generate the same level of return, the risk of equities is generally lower, especially compared to futures, forwards, and FOREX transaction. The liquidity of equities is also generally higher, especially when compared to venture capital, LBO, or real estate investments. The transaction cost of equities is generally lower, especially compared to the tradings of private equities or collections.

Common stock (and also preferred stock) is an asset class that fits almost everyone. To be clear, I am not saying that a specific type of stock can fit everyone. That is not possible. Stocks and their derived assets, such as ETFs, vary dramatically in terms of their own characteristics.

The "blue chips" common stocks and some preferred stocks have very low volatility and deliver stable, yet low and slow, returns. These stocks are more appropriate for investors who cannot afford significant loss and are not pursuing sizable gains.

This is vice versa for high return stocks. The small market capitalizations stocks at the growth phase can easily double their stock prices in a few months, or lose half of its value. They might not pay significant dividends either. Investors holding such stocks on their accounts might see their assets grow exponentially, or lose a big piece of value. *To conclude, not all stocks fit you, but there are almost always some stocks that are appropriate in terms of your need of return, as well as your risk tolerance.*

Stilleven Jobs: But as you said in the two tables above, there are many other options. Like bonds, futures, and so on. Is equity the best investment asset for us?

Professor Dong: First of all, please use caution when using the term "option" in finance, because it stands for a specific type of specific financial assets.

In a nut shell, equity is the most appropriate financial asset for entry-level non-professionals.

The path for investments is from pure ETF investments to equity investments with single stock picking, and then to FOREX, bond, and futures investments. FOREX stands for foreign exchange investments that will be introduced in *Volume Three* of this book series.

In general, ETF investments are the least time consuming and require least amount of knowledge and experience on investments. Investments with single individual stock selection are more time consuming, and requires more skills and knowledge of the related methods. FOREX and futures investments are even more time consuming and more appropriate for people who have handled their investments for at least one year. In terms of the gains, the ETFs are usually regarded as more conservative, and the hope for huge and quick return are more possible in the FOREX and futures markets than in the ETF market.

4 WHY MUTUAL FUNDS ARE NOT GOOD INSTRUMENTS

Baroque Omaha: Should I invest by myself? Aren't institutional investors or professional investors more capable of generating a profit for me?

Professor Dong: You should do equity investments by yourself. Investing in mutual funds, hedge funds, or pension funds managed by professional investors ultimately generates significantly lower returns compared to making an investment by yourself.

Asking your financial advisor to invest for you generates an even lower return when compared to a "do it yourself" strategy on average.

Individual investors who invest in mutual funds, hedge funds, and pension funds receive their portfolio passively. There is no "one-of-a-kind" investment for individual investors[3]. Therefore, the return target, lock-up period, risk, volatility, liquidity, or tax of the fund might not fit your exact personal needs. You cannot determine the fate of your investment.

Moselle Omaha: I think you are right. No one understands my need better than me. But how come I can do a better job than the pros?

Professor Dong: Yes. For a thorough comparison of investing by yourself or investing via professional funds and advisors, please refer to the book *The Hedge Fund Mirage: The Illusion of Big Money and Why It's too good to Be True* by

---

[3] If you are very rich, thing might be different. Asset management companies as well as financial advisors call wealthy clients "high net worth (HNW)" investors. They might offer the HNWs more "one-of-a-kind" portfolio that is tailored to the need of each wealthy client. The threshold of being an HNW is usually 1 million U.S. dollar of *liquid* assets.

Simon Lack, CFA. He worked for JPMorgan for twenty-three years and sat on JPMorgan's investment committee, allocating over $1 billion to hedge fund managers. He also founded the JPMorgan Incubator Funds. Even he as a very successful fund manager cannot guarantee better performance than the market average over time.

Mutual funds, hedge funds, and pension funds frequently have minimum investment requirements. *The worst part are their fees*, such as the management fee, account fee, paper document fee, transfer fee, trust fee, consulting fee, front-load fee, and end-load fee. These fees easily go beyond 5% of your principal.

Worse still are the incentive charges of these funds: common practice in the financial industry is 20% of the investment profit, yet 0% of the loss. When your investment gains a profit, the fund would grab 20% from it; when you incur a loss, you are fully responsible for it. Such asymmetric payoff mechanisms lead fund managers to invest in an aggressive and less cautious manner because higher risk might bring higher return for them.

These fee arrangements will not be easily recognized. They are usually buried in the small-size printed footnotes of the fund brochure.

In other words, when you invest $100 in a mutual fund, you would pay a $5 fee immediately and only $95 is truly used to be put into your investment. Suppose the investment creates a gain of 7%. The profit that belongs to you is 80% of 7%, which is 5.6%. Twenty percent of the 7% is paid to the fund manager as an incentive fee. So your account is only growing by $95*5.6%, which is $5.32. Your end-of-period balance is $100.32. Now you know the game: while the account report says the fund investments have gained a 7% return, the return that you end up receive is only 0.32%.

Even worse is that if you incur a loss, say 7%, you will absorb the full loss. In this case your $95 investment capital will lose $95*7%, which is $6.65. You end up receive $95-$6.65=$88.35. So your real loss from your initial $100 investment is 11.65%.

Stilleven Jobs: OK. This is truly the worst. So how about I use an investment advisor to invest, instead of investing my money with the funds that you have just mentioned?

Professor Dong: *Worse than "the part even worse than the worst" is*, when you make your investment advisor invest in these funds for you, you are peeled twice! Your financial advisor will first charge a service fee from your capital, and then will use the leftover money to purchase funds, which will charge you another layer of service fee and incentive fee.

To summarize, when you invest by yourself and receive a gain or loss of 7%, your $100 become $107 or $93; when you invest in a mutual/hedge/pension fund and receive a gain or loss of 7%, your $100 become $100.32 or $88.35. If you make your financial advisor invest in those funds for you, the return is even lower.

Wanna Buffet: But these investment advisors and professional investment banks are more knowledgeable and have more information on what stocks to purchase. I don't have a fraction of the knowledge that they have.

Professor Dong: I would like to cite and quote some facts from the most respected finance book *A Random Walk down Wall Street*. More than 1.5 million copies of this book have been sold and its author, Dr. Burton Malkiel, is a Professor of Economics at Princeton University and the former Dean of Yale University, School of Management. His book uses massive amount of serious mathematical proofs and statistical data to test, evaluate, and review various types of stock investment strategies.

Pages 160 to 182 of the 2015 Edition of his book use numerous fresh data and track records to provide a thorough review of "professional investment institutions in the United States".

Page 180: In 2014, only 55.8% of professional investment funds that focus on large cap stocks beat the benchmark; only 52.8% of professional investment funds that focus on small cap stocks beat the benchmark. Dr. Burton Malkiel cited these data from Standard and Poor's 2014 Report.

Page 181: From 1970 to 2013, the amount of actively managed professional stock investment funds decreased from 358 to 84. There were 76.5% professional stock investment funds that failed to survive. Among the 23.5% professional institutions that fortunately survived, twenty-two of them realize returns lower than the benchmark by 0-1%, and eighteen of them generate returns lower than the benchmark by 1-2%.

Therefore, asking "professional investment managers" to invest for you has a measly 50-50 chance to outperform the return that you can generate if you do it by yourself.

Unfortunately, the incentive fee, profit split, service fee, and management fee charged by those professional investors per year would make your return 2.5% lower than investing by yourself on average. This difference would be 63.86% in twenty years, which is $(1+2.5\%)^{20}-1$.

Moselle Omaha: Don't institutional funds and professional investors have access to stocks that individuals don't understand or can't invest in? They have more choices, don't they?

Professor Dong: That is largely not true. I explained this when I was answering your questions about ETFs. By investing in an ETF, individual investors can do a better job than institutional investors. Exchange-Traded Funds allow individual investors to have access to the companies that you cannot invest as an individual or the companies that you do not understand as a non-professional.

Therefore, the choices that institutional investors face is largely the same as what individual investors face. The components and balance of an ETF is usually so carefully allocated that the individual non-professional investors do not need to understand the single assets.

You also need to note that because of the rigid legal regulations and requirements set by law, professional investors in asset management companies frequently act irrationally and reluctantly. For example, if the brochure of a fund claims that the fund will only invest in Standard and Poor 100 component stocks, the fund will miss many good investment opportunities.

Another example reflects the common practice in U.S. pension fund management. If a fund is required to invest in bonds whose credit ratings are no lower than AA, the fund must immediately sell off its current position on a bond if the bond is downgraded to AA-. However, because of this most recent downgrade, the bond price is likely to take a huge plunge. This is obviously not a good time to sell off. A more reasonable transaction tactic is to wait until the panic in the market fades away and the price adjusts to a higher level.

If individual investors are managing and investing by themselves, they can completely avoid such unreasonable, rigid restriction in funds and can control investment decisions by themselves.

Stilleven Jobs: I see. I like the flexibility of do-it-yourself investment. But the size of my assets is really small. How do I play along with the large professional institutions?

Professor Dong: There is a very famous principle among professional investors and institutional funds: size is the enemy of performance. This brings an extra headache for investors when choosing funds to invest. Younger and smaller funds might bring higher return, but they lack experienced and consistent performance in the history with different market environments – from good time such as 2013 to bad time such as 2008.

However, larger and more matured funds tend to suffer from their size. A larger size means it is more and more difficult for a fund to hire high-competence fund managers as the fund grows, and existing fund managers are less and less excited to cover more research and analysis demanded by the growth of the fund.

Larger size also means extra performance difficulty: when a fund manager wants to purchase or sell a stock for the fund, millions of dollars are usually involved in the transaction. This large order can very quickly absorb all of the liquidity in the market and bring the price up or down dramatically.

For a stock whose liquidity is below average, an order from a fund can bring its price up or down by more than 20%, and the fund ends up with a high and not-profitable average entry price. This also means a very low selling price.

Another significant downside to professional investors and institutional funds is the short-term performance pressure. Funds and other asset management service providers need to report the fund performance to their client at least quarterly, sometimes more frequently than that. The market value of mutual funds is even reported on a daily basis. Fund managers then inevitably act shortsightedly to generate a good-looking report to smooth the otherwise upset investors.

For example, a fund incurs significant loss on one stock during the current period, worrying the investor to the point of possible withdrawal. The fund manager sells some of its currently profitable positions to cover the loss to avoid a report that shows negative return. However, the assets being sold are in fact gaining steadily and it is certainly not reasonable to sell them.

Last but not the least, funds and fund managers always garner attention from the media and investors. This would lead their biased investments to "safer" and "more-respected" stocks.

In this case, funds and fund managers do not want to express any adverse opinions on the stocks issued by respectful companies, and they understand that they would take the sole responsibility of their decisions if they pick unknown assets.

When fund managers buy Boeing stock and incur a loss, investors usually blame the company and ask "what's wrong with Boeing?" But when fund managers buy WNC (Wabash, a firm that produces truck trailers and its stock is in the small cap category) and incur a loss, investors usually blame the manager and ask "what's wrong with you?" In such case, while fund managers understand herding behavior might not be reasonable, they might still choose to do so by following consensus and buy "safe" stocks like Boeing.

Stilleven Jobs: So, you're saying that I can invest in market indexes and make better profits than professional investors? Even though I don't understand stocks?

Professor Dong: Yes. This is not just my personal conclusion. This suggestion is the unanimous conclusion from numerous professors in U.S. finance academia, a conclusion reached after reviewing countless historical return data and trading strategies.

Furthermore, if you pick individual stocks by yourself rather than simply investing in a stock market index, your profit is likely to be higher than professional investors.

Peter Lynch, the only investment guru whose name is aligned with Warren Buffett, also recommends that individual investors invest by themselves. He managed the Magellan Fund for thirteen years and concentrated his wisdom in his book *Beating the Street*, the Top Five Best Seller among Amazon business books. From pages 15 to 35, he explains why professional investors do not generate as good of a performance as amateur individual investors. In fact, Lynch, as one of the top two most successful investors in the history of the U.S. financial market, has spent his lifetime advocating that people should invest by themselves.

Wanna Buffet: But the commercials and mail-in flyers I received from funds and asset managers claim they make very good returns. Are you telling me that that they're lying?

Professor Dong: Yes and no. They might be playing the "asset weight" game. I would like to use the following example to unveil the secret of the professional investment and funds industry.

Suppose you invested $1,000 to buy a mutual fund at the beginning of 2015, and the fund gained 56% return in that year. At the end of 2015, your account balance became $1,560. You were very satisfied. At the beginning of 2016, you spent another $1,000 to buy this fund. At that moment, your investing capital became $2,560. However, the fund incurred a loss of 40% in 2016. At the end, your account balance become $2,560×(1-40%)=$1,536.

However, the advisors of this fund at this moment can claim that "our fund realizes an annual average return of 8% in the year 2015 and the year 2016, beating the market index by 3%", and their way of calculating such a return is:

$$\frac{56\% + (-40\%)}{2} = 8\%$$

However, you as the investor of this fund invested $2,000 but only got $1,536 back. You have, in fact, incurred a 23.2% loss!

We cannot assert that the way the fund presents their return is not correct, or the fund is dishonest, yet their way of calculation does hide the fact that you gain less but lose more.

Moselle Omaha: But aren't there many outstanding professional investors in the U.S., such as Peter Lynch and Warren Buffett that you just mentioned? Can't I just invest in their funds?

Professor Dong: The stock price of Berkshire Hathaway (NYSE: BRK.A), which is managed by Buffett, was traded at $216,130 as of April 13, 2016. This is actually a relatively low price compared to its previous high point of $229,374 per share. This is not an individual investor-friendly price.

Peter Lynch retired 25 years ago. The two of them are investment gurus; yet you can't just meet with them and have them manage your assets. When you're facing a list of thousands of funds and fund managers, you can never identify which of the strange names belong to the next Warren Buffett.

In terms of fund and asset manager selection, I would like to quote Peter Lynch's statement in *Beating the Street* from pages 67 to 68: "Some people take last year's biggest winner, the one at the top of the Lipper list of 1-year achievers, and buy that fund. This is particularly foolish. The 1-year winner tends to be a fund managed by someone who bet on one industry or one kind of company in a hot sector and got lucky…alas, this picking future winners from past performance doesn't seem to work even when you use a 3-year or 5-year record…in the end you would have lagged the S&P 500 by 2.05 percent."

What does he mean by lagging the market by 2.05% every year? It means that in ten years, this "picking the best fund" strategy return would be $(1+2.05\%)^{10}-1=22.4983\%$ less than the return of direct investments by individual investor themselves.

As a matter of fact, simply buying the ETF that tracks the return of Standard and Poor's 500 index[4], the average annual return is as high as 9.50%. Please see the table[5] below. The first column is the S & P 500 return, the second is the 3-month Treasury Bill return, and the third is the 10-year Treasury Bond return.

Arithmetic Average

1928-2015	11.41%	3.49%	5.23%
1966-2015	11.01%	4.97%	7.12%
2006-2015	9.03%	1.16%	5.16%

Geometric Average

1928-2015	9.50%	3.45%	4.96%
1966-2015	9.61%	4.92%	6.71%
2006-2015	7.25%	1.14%	4.71%

Moselle Omaha: Lower than the general market performance is not something I want to see. Now I do want to try a little bit of investments by myself. Where should I start?

Professor Dong: Well. The next chapter starts to take you into the door.

Image yourself learning how to play soccer. Here is a reasonable learning path: you first learn the rules and facts - what a soccer ball is like; how many players there are in each team; what "handball" means, etc.

Then you learn the basic skills: how to stop a ball, how to pass, how to

---

[4] The ticker of that ETF is SPY.
[5] Cited from pages.stern.nyu.edu/~adamodar/New_Home_Page/datafile/ histretSP.html

protect yourself, etc.

Finally, you learn the specific tactics and strategies: different roles in a team; how to systematically defend; how to find the most effective way of scoring a goal.

Learning investments is exactly the same.

The next chapter starts by introducing the rules in the game, as well as the basic facts.

The leftover chapters in this book discuss the methods of investments in general, as well as the knowledge of risk management.

Volume Two of this book series delves into the detailed tactics and strategies.

5 PREPARATIONS AND JARGONS

Stilleven Jobs: What is the fundamental meaning of a stock?

Professor Dong: A stock is a share of ownership of the firm that issues the sock. When a firm, say, Walt Disney, issues stocks and you purchase a share of them, a piece of the firm is owned by you. You can enjoy the firm's profit and earnings, but you are also responsible for the firm's loss.

Nowadays, all stock transactions are paperless. Most of the brokerage companies only send paper-based statements and stock transaction receipts when particularly requested by clients. And frequently there is a fee attached to that. When you buy a stock, you do not hold a price of "paper stock" in hand. It is only a conceptual record in your account. The stock that you are holding is simply a confirmation email, or a short message sent to your smart phone.

Wanna Buffet: What's a portfolio?

Professor Dong: A portfolio is a basket of assets that an investor holds. For example, an investor's current portfolio can include dozens of stocks, ETFs, some options, a house, and so on.

Baroque Omaha: How do I select among the brokerage companies?

Professor Dong: There are two types of brokers: full service brokers and discount brokers. Full service brokers provide many "professional research and advising" services, such as stock recommendations, stock rating and picking, financing, short-term loans, etc. The cost is a lot higher for using full service brokers. Seldom do investors with short term investment span and small-size capital use full service brokers.

The discount brokers, on the other hand, provide only stock facts and data, as well as transaction order execution for investors. The cost is a lot lower. This is the type of broker that most of the individual investors use in the U.S. I also recommend this type of broker. The commission is usually around $7.5 per transaction, and some can even be $0.

In a nut shell, full service brokers provide data, suggestions, and execution; discount brokers provide data and execution. As I explained earlier, professional investors do not do any better of a job than amateur investors, and their investment suggestions on stock picking are almost always concurrent, rather than in advance.

For facts about brokerage companies, you can go to various search engines on the Internet and key in "stock broker comparison" to see a list of ratings and reviews.

The following list presents the best online brokers 2016 rated by the stockbrokers.com[6]. Each individual broker was assessed on 295 unique variables. Full length reviews for each broker can be found on their respective review pages:

Capital One Investing, stockbrokers.com/review/sharebuilder
Charles Schwab, stockbrokers.com/review/charlesschwab
E*TRADE, stockbrokers.com/review/charlesschwab
Fidelity Investments, stockbrokers.com/review/fidelityinvestments
Firstrade, stockbrokers.com/review/firstrade
Lightspeed Trading, stockbrokers.com/review/lightspeedtrading
Merrill Edge, stockbrokers.com/review/merrilledge
OptionsHouse, stockbrokers.com/review/optionshouse
Scottrade, stockbrokers.com/review/scottrade
SogoTrade, stockbrokers.com/review/sogotrade
TD Ameritrade, stockbrokers.com/review/tdameritrade
TradeKing, stockbrokers.com/review/tradeking
TradeStation, stockbrokers.com/review/tradestation

Stilleven Jobs: How do I open an account?

Professor Dong: All the brokers I have heard of offer full online application processes. You can search their website and start the application process, which usually takes less than thirty minutes. You can deposit funds via checking account, debit card, or ACH transfer during the application process; or you can always deposit later and keep an empty account at the beginning.

---

[6] The author does not have any beneficiary, monetary or non-monetary, relationship with stockbroker.com or the rated companies that affects the descriptions above. The author has brokerage account associated with optionshouse.

Baroque Omaha: How do I open an account if I am not a U.S. citizen or a U.S. permanent resident?

Professor Dong: In the U.S., when you open a brokerage account for equity investments, you need to provide the social security number, unless you open an international account. Investors in or outside of the United States who do not have a U.S. social security number might be able to take this option, However, there are strict restrictions on the eligibility of opening an international account, mainly for tax reasons.

Moselle Omaha: How do I link my retirement accounts to an equity investment account?

Professor Dong: When you open the investment account with a broker, you can usually choose the type of the account: individual, joint, IRA, Roth IRA, etc. You can also change the type of the account.

Baroque Omaha: Please explain the tax impact of my equity investment.

Professor Dong: I would like to quote some paragraphs from the article *Investment Tax Basics for All Investors* by Neil O'Hara, retrieved from Investopedia.

"The federal government taxes not only investment income - dividends, interest, rent on real estate, etc. - but also realized capital gains. The taxman is smart, too; investors cannot escape by investing indirectly through mutual funds, exchange-traded funds, REITs or limited partnerships. For tax purposes, these entities are transparent."

"Companies pay dividends out of after-tax profits, which means the taxman has already taken a cut. That's why shareholders get a break - a preferential tax rate of 15% on 'qualified dividends' if the company is domiciled in the U.S. or in a country that has a double-taxation treaty with the U.S. acceptable to the IRS. Non-qualified dividends - paid by other foreign companies or entities that receive non-qualified income (a dividend paid from interest on bonds held by a mutual fund, for example) - are taxed at regular income tax rates, which are typically higher. "

"Uncle Sam's levy on realized capital gains depends on how long an investor held the security. The tax rate on long-term (more than one year) gains is 15%, except for high-income taxpayers (in 2013, $400,000 for singles, $450,000 for married couples) who must pay 20%. High-rate taxpayers will typically pay the healthcare surtax as well, for an all-in rate of 23.8%."

"Short-term (less than one year of valid holding period) capital gains are taxed at regular income tax rates."

"Investors may offset capital gains against capital losses realized either in the same tax year or carried forward from previous years. Individuals may deduct up to $3,000 of net capital losses against other taxable income each year, too, while any losses in excess of the allowance are available until either offset against gains in future years or amortized against the annual allowance."

"Investors can minimize their capital gains tax liability by harvesting tax losses. If one or more stocks in a portfolio drops below an investor's cost basis, the investor can sell and realize a capital loss for tax purposes, which will be available to offset capital gains either in the same or a future year."

Baroque Omaha: What is an ADR?

Professor Dong: An American Depositary Receipt, or ADR, is a certificate issued by a bank in the United States representing some shares (or one share) of a foreign stock that is traded in the U.S. stock market. ADRs are denominated in U.S. dollars and are traded the same way as the domestic stock in America. In other words, it is a convenient way for investors in the U.S. market to invest in foreign stocks without requiring a sophisticated knowledge of foreign markets or economies, or requiring a foreign stock investment account.

Wanna Buffet: What is a ticker?

Professor Dong: The ticker of a stock is the symbol that you key into the trading platform. It is usually a string of letters consistent with the firm's name or major business. For example, the ticker for AT&T is T; the ticker for Coca Cola is KO; the ticker for Walmart is WMT; the ticker for the global crude oil ETF is OIL; the ticker for New Oriental Education Group is EDU; the ticker for an agribusiness ETF is MOO.

Moselle Omaha: What is an ETF? Why it is a type of important asset?

Professor Dong: Please refer to Chapter Two, if you have not read it before reading this current chapter.

Wanna Buffet: What do long and short mean?

Professor Dong: Long means to buy, and short means to sell. For example, "long DD" means to buy the DuPont stock; "short JNJ" means to sell Johnson & Johnson stock. DD and JNJ are the stocks' tickers.

Stilleven Jobs: What is a position?

Professor Dong: A position is a currently active transaction that you opened a while ago. For example, "a long $3,000 BA position" means that you spent $3,000 to buy the Boeing stock. "A long 60 shares BA position" means that you are currently holding 60 shares of Boeing stock.

A long position would gain profit if the stock price goes up, and would incur loss if the stock price goes down. A short position would gain profit if the stock price goes down, and would incur loss if the stock price goes up.

Wanna Buffet: I am having difficulty with the idea of a short position. You are saying that short position means an open position to sell something. But my understanding is that, when you sell something, it happens at a point of time, rather than during a period of time. How come it can be the case that I *am selling* something? I thought I just sell the stock that I used to hold, and I then no longer hold it.

Professor Dong: Beginners usually have a hard time understanding the concept of "being short". Please keep in mind that you do not need to first hold an asset and then take a short position on it. You can be short an asset when you do not have any position on it. Here's how it works: you borrow a stock that you expect to decline in price from a broker, and then sell it at the current (high) market price. If you are correct and the price of the stock does decline, you enter the market, purchase it back at a lower market price, and return it to the broker. The difference between the high selling price and low buying price is the holder's profit.

In a real transaction, there is no need to go through the process discussed above. Simply click on "sell" next to a stock whose price you think will decrease and you have opened a short position. If the price of the asset does decrease, you would realize a gain when you close the short position.

Moselle Omaha: What is an order?

Professor Dong: An order is a command to buy or sell. There are two main types of orders: market and limit. Market orders take the current market price and immediately open a position. Limit orders are the pre-set price levels that "wait" until stocks move and trigger an open position. Market orders can open a position without uncertainty, yet the entry price might not be ideal – too high for a long and too low for a short. Limit orders, however, have the uncertainty that a position might not be triggered, and once open, the market environment may have already changed[7]. However, limit orders can obtain a better[8] entry price.

For example, the following figure shows a limit order of NIKE (NKE) which allows the input of a desired open price determined by the investor:

---

[7] For example, the original trend no longer exists. Or some sudden events changed the fundamental aspect of the asset.

[8] Better in this case means that for a long position, the price that you pay to buy is lower; for a short position, the price that you receive to sell is higher.

The following figure shows a market order which does not allow the input of a desired open price determined by the investor. The investor can only take the current market trading price of the undergoing price. Usually, such type of orders is filled[9] very quickly.

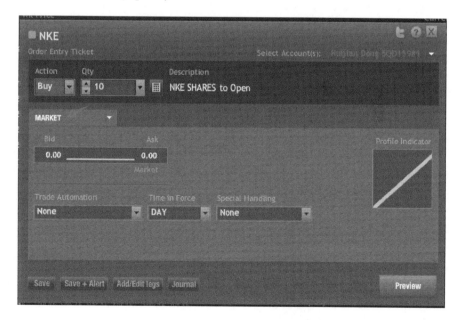

---

[9] Being filled means the order is executed by the brokerage firm.

Baroque Omaha: What is paper money?

Professor Dong: It is the virtual money provided by a broker to allow investors to study and practice trading on a real platform. It is simply a conceptual idea that does not have real monetary value. It is not blended with the investor's real cash balance.

Stilleven Jobs: What is total return?

Professor Dong: Total return is also called holding period return. For stock investors, total return can be generated from two sources: dividend income and capital gain income.

Wanna Buffet: What is a dividend?

Professor Dong: A firm generates revenue from its major operating business, supplementary business, and extraordinary business. After its revenue is subtracted by cost of production, management, depreciation, interest paid to the lender, and tax, the firm reaches its net income, which is the firm's profit.

A firm will keep part of the profit for future replacement, development, and expansion. The firm will distribute the other part of the profit to its owners as the "income of doing business". This part is called the dividend.

Moselle Omaha: What is capital gain?

Professor Dong: Capital gain is also called capital appreciation. If you buy a share of a firm's stock at a price of $10 and sell it at $15, your capital gain is $5. Capital gain comes from the appreciation of a firm's value. It might be because of a better future perspective of the firm, a better position in business competition, a special technology or monopolistic power, etc.

Stilleven Jobs: What is net return?

Professor Dong: It is the total return subtracted by the transaction cost. Explicitly, transaction cost includes commission paid to the broker; implicitly, transaction cost also includes the bid-ask price paid to the broker.

Wanna Buffet: What is bid price, ask price, and bid-ask spread?

Professor Dong: Bid price is the price you receive when you sell an asset. Ask price is the price you pay when you purchase an asset. Ask price is always higher than bid price, and the difference, which is called the bid-ask spread, is the profit earned by the brokers.

The pattern of price quotes from brokers is usually [bid/ask].

For example, you opened a long position at [$5.38, $5.40] and closed the position at [$6.44, $6.45]. Your profit per share is the sell price at close subtracted by the buy price at open, which is $6.44-$5.40, or a $1.04 gain.

Similarly, if you opened a long position at [$5.38, $5.40] and closed the position at [$3.89, $3.95], your loss per share is the sell price at close minus the buy price at open, which is $3.89-$5.40, or a $1.51 loss.

Here's another example. Say that you opened a short position at [$5.38, $5.40] and closed the position at [$6.44, $6.45]. Your loss per share is the buy price at close minus the sell price at open, which is $5.38-$6.45, or a $1.07 loss.

Lastly, if you opened a short position at [$5.38, $5.40] and closed the position at [$3.89, $3.95], your profit per share is the buy price at close minus the sell price at open, which is $5.38-$3.95, or a $1.43 gain.

6 INVESTMENT PLANNING

Stilleven Jobs: What steps do I need to take to invest in U.S. equity?

Professor Dong: First, identify your reason for investing and your needs. Rather than vaguely saying "I want to make money," you need to measure the size of your current investable asset and your specific demand on return and on liquidity. This can help set up your goal of investments and your investment style. For example, "I have $50,000 that I can use to buy stocks. I hope I can make $8,000 out of it in two years to pay off my student loan and I hope I can make $50,000 out of it to support my older kid's higher education after 15 years." This way you can gauge what your required return per year in the first two years will be:

$$\sqrt{1 + \frac{8000}{50000}} - 1 = 7.7\%$$

You can also gauge what your required return per year *after* the first two years will be:

$$\sqrt[13]{1 + \frac{50000}{50000}} - 1 = 5.48\%$$

A detailed collection of calculation templates that you can use is presented later in this Chapter.

Next, you need to identify your risk tolerance after understanding your goal of return. Given the return requirement, your risk tolerance should match the level of risk of the assets which can bring you the return you are pursuing.

Risk tolerance is determined by the lower of two factors: the risk you are willing to take, and the risk you are able to take. Let's continue the example. In the first two years if you demand 7.7% annual return, this would require you to invest in assets that might cause you to lose $5.65 per each $100 investment in a year, hypothetically. You need, at this moment, to gauge if your current situation can afford such a loss, and if you are comfortable with such uncertainty. In this chapter I also provide a precise table in which you may compare the return with the corresponding possibility of capital loss.

Next, you need to determine your investment type and style. For example, would you aggressively invest, or conservatively? Is your chief goal a steady cash flow, or a large capital appreciation? Do you need to frequently pull money out of the investment account, or can you make a long term investment that is not interrupted? If your answers to these questions are mixed, then what would be the ratio of different styles? In Chapter Seven I have a thorough example of available strategies that you can use to determine your investment style.

Finally, you need to take action on preparing your investment capital. It is human nature to maintain the status quo and not put thoughts into action. This is also the reason why successful people are always a very small portion of the population.

Many, if not too many, people summarize the reason for their current financial stress with: "I should have started saving by investing in stocks earlier". The average annual return of the Standard & Poor's 500 index from 1928 to 2014 is approximately 10%. If an investor plans to invest $50,000 in stock but only takes action on the real investment after half a year, she or he on average loses:

$$50000 \times \frac{1}{2} \times 365 \times \left(\sqrt[365]{1 + 10\%} - 1 \right) = \$2383.07$$

In other words, if you plan to invest $50,000 in stock but you did not take action immediately, the cost of delay is $13.06 every day. It is expensive to be lazy!

Moselle Omaha: How do you compute future gains for a single cash flow?

Professor Dong: First of all, single cash flow refers to the cash flow that only occurs once in the present and once in the future, such as if you invest now and withdraw in the future. It contrasts with a multiple cash flow type, which involves many cash flows that occur periodically or irregularly, such as if you invest every month.

The formula is:

$$Future\ gains = Current\ Deposit \times (1 + return\ per\ period)^{Number\ of\ periods}$$

So in Excel, for any cell in a spreadsheet, key in:

=current deposit*(1+return per period)^number of periods

For example, if you invest $2000 now in the stock market and you expect the annual return to be 10%, after 5 years, your account balance would be:

=2000*(1+10%)^5

In Excel when you hit enter, the output should be 3221.02.

Please note that the unit of measurement for the return period must be consistent with that of the measurement for the number of periods. If you invest $50,000 now in the stock market and you expect the monthly return to be 1%, after 3 years, your account balance would be:

=50000*(1+1%)^36

In Excel when you hit enter, the output should be 71538.44.

It is incorrect to calculate the future gains in the following way, as the return is based on *month* whereas the number of periods is based on the count of *years*.

=50000*(1+1%)^3

Baroque Omaha: How do you compute the current capital demand for a single cash flow?

Professor Dong: The formula is:

$$Current\ Capital\ Demand = Future\ Target\ Return/(1 + return\ per\ period)^{Number\ of\ periods}$$

So in Excel, for any cell in a spreadsheet, key in:

=Future Target Return/(1+return per period)^number of periods

For example, if you want to receive a return of $8000 after 15 years, and the annual return is expected to be 7%, then you currently need to invest:

=8000/(1+7%)^15

In Excel when you hit enter, the output should be 2899.568.

Stilleven Jobs: How do you compute future gains for multiple equal and even-frequency cash flows?

Professor Dong: For example, you invest $500 at the *end* of every month for 3 years, and the average monthly return of stocks is 0.88%. After 3 years, you would receive $21069.72. The way to calculate that is by entering into Excel:

$$=FV(0.88\%,3*12,-500,0,0)$$

The 3*12 in the Excel formula represents that there are 12 months in a year and that in 3 years there will be 36 periods that will generate a per period return of 0.88%.

As another example, you invest $500 at the *beginning* of every month for 3 years, and the average monthly return of stocks is 0.88%. After 3 years, you would receive $21255.13. The way to calculate that is by entering into Excel:

$$=FV(0.88\%,3*12,-500,0,1)$$

In addition, say you invest $2500 at the *beginning* of every quarter for 8 years, and the average quarterly return of stocks is 2.91%. After 8 years, you would receive $132,973.79. The way to calculate that is by entering into Excel:

$$=FV(2.91\%,8*4,-2500,0,1)$$

The 8*4 in the Excel formula represents that there are 4 quarters in a year and that in 8 years there will be 32 periods that will generate a per period return of 2.91%.

Wanna Buffet: How do you compute current capital demand for multiple equal and even cash flows?

Professor Dong: Say, for example, that you would need to withdraw $5000 at the beginning of each year in the next 6 years to support your child's education. The annual return is 8% in the stock market. How many assets do you need to invest in now in the stock market?

You need to invest $24963.55 now. The way to calculate that is by entering into Excel:

$$=PV(8\%,6, 5000,0,1)$$

In fact, the output of this function in Excel is negative. That implies that the $24963.55 is a current cash outflow.

Baroque Omaha: How do you calculate the annual return rate demand?

Professor Dong: The formula is:

$$\text{annual return rate demand} = \sqrt[\text{the number of years of investment}]{1 + \frac{Capital\ appreciation\ by\ demand}{your\ initial\ investment}} - 1$$

To compute the outcome, in Excel please enter:

=(1 + Capital appreciation by demand / your initial investment)^(1/the number of years of investment)-1

For example, an investor has $50,000 that can be used to buy stocks, and this investor hopes that s/he can make $8,000 out of it in three years. By applying the formula above, the annual return demand is:

$$\sqrt[3]{1 + \frac{8000}{50000}} - 1 = 7.7\%$$

To compute the outcome, in Excel please enter:

=(1+ 8000/50000)^(1/3)-1

Moselle Omaha: How can I compute my lifetime investment and expenditure?

Professor Dong: Let's say, for example, that you are 25 years old now and you plan to retire when you are 62. After retirement you plan to withdraw $1000 out of your investment account at the beginning of each month to support your living expenditure. You expect that you will have 20 more years of life after retirement. The monthly return from the stock market is 0.85%. How much do you need to invest every month at the end of each month from now?

Starting from the current moment, you will need to invest $20.93 at the end of each month, until you retire after 37 years. To calculate that, in Excel please enter:

=PMT(0.85%, 37*12,0, -PV(0.85%,20*12,1000,0,1),0)

For practice, please work on the following question:

Hypothetically, you are 35 years old now and your kids will go to private high school and college after 10 years. By that time you will need to withdraw $50000 at the beginning of every year out of your investment account to support your kids. You need to make this withdrawal for 8 years. You expect that they will graduate from college when you are 53 years old. The annual stock market return is 9%. How much do you need to invest at the end of every year, starting now?

The answer is, beginning now, you need to invest $19854.47 every year at the end of each year, until you are 45 years old. The way to calculate that is by entering into Excel:

=PMT(9%, 10,0, -PV(9%,8,50000,0,1),0)

Baroque Omaha: How do you obtain the relationship between risk and return?

Professor Dong: The following chart is based on the trailing-120-month risk-return relationship of the Standard and Poor 500 Index as of February 14, 2016. This table covers the daily risk-return relationship from February 14, 2006 to February 14, 2016. This period includes two expansionary periods, two recessionary periods, and two normal periods. Therefore, it is relatively reliable. The two expansionary cycles covered are the 2006-2007 boom and the 2012-2014 boom, while the two recessionary cycles covered are the 2008 sub-prime mortgage crisis and the 2011 European debt crisis. The two normal return periods are the 2009-2010 recovery period and the 2015 staggered growth period.

Investors using this table should understand that it is used to gauge the market average risk-return relationship. This table does not guarantee the return, or the risk.

Investors using this table should also understand that the risk-return relationship evolves dynamically, though it is relatively stable. For a quarterly updated risk-return relationship, please contact the author.

In addition, please review in the previous questions how to calculate annual return demand.

Stilleven Jobs: Can you show us the table?

Professor Dong:
  Column A: Annual Return Demand of Investor
  Column B: Corresponding Expected Daily Return
  Column C: The Lowest Daily Loss at 1% Probability Level

Column D: The Risk-Return Reward Relationship

A	B	C	D	A	B	C	D
1.2857%	0.0035%	0.0656%	0.61100	23.7957%	0.0585%	8.1268%	0.00670
1.4707%	0.0040%	0.1389%	0.33567	24.0217%	0.0590%	8.2001%	0.00664
1.6560%	0.0045%	0.2122%	0.23140	24.2481%	0.0595%	8.2734%	0.00658
1.8417%	0.0050%	0.2854%	0.17655	24.4750%	0.0600%	8.3467%	0.00652
2.0277%	0.0055%	0.3587%	0.14272	24.7022%	0.0605%	8.4200%	0.00647
2.2141%	0.0060%	0.4320%	0.11977	24.9298%	0.0610%	8.4932%	0.00641
2.4008%	0.0065%	0.5053%	0.10318	25.1579%	0.0615%	8.5665%	0.00635
2.5878%	0.0070%	0.5786%	0.09063	25.3864%	0.0620%	8.6398%	0.00630
2.7752%	0.0075%	0.6519%	0.08080	25.6153%	0.0625%	8.7131%	0.00625
2.9629%	0.0080%	0.7251%	0.07289	25.8446%	0.0630%	8.7864%	0.00620
3.1510%	0.0085%	0.7984%	0.06640	26.0743%	0.0635%	8.8597%	0.00615
3.3394%	0.0090%	0.8717%	0.06096	26.3045%	0.0640%	8.9329%	0.00609
3.5281%	0.0095%	0.9450%	0.05635	26.5350%	0.0645%	9.0062%	0.00605
3.7172%	0.0100%	1.0183%	0.05239	26.7660%	0.0650%	9.0795%	0.00600
3.9067%	0.0105%	1.0916%	0.04894	26.9974%	0.0655%	9.1528%	0.00595
4.0965%	0.0110%	1.1648%	0.04593	27.2293%	0.0660%	9.2261%	0.00590
4.2866%	0.0115%	1.2381%	0.04326	27.4615%	0.0665%	9.2994%	0.00586
4.4771%	0.0120%	1.3114%	0.04089	27.6942%	0.0670%	9.3727%	0.00581
4.6679%	0.0125%	1.3847%	0.03876	27.9273%	0.0675%	9.4459%	0.00576
4.8591%	0.0130%	1.4580%	0.03684	28.1608%	0.0680%	9.5192%	0.00572
5.0506%	0.0135%	1.5313%	0.03511	28.3948%	0.0685%	9.5925%	0.00568
5.2424%	0.0140%	1.6046%	0.03353	28.6291%	0.0690%	9.6658%	0.00563
5.4347%	0.0145%	1.6778%	0.03208	28.8639%	0.0695%	9.7391%	0.00559
5.6272%	0.0150%	1.7511%	0.03076	29.0992%	0.0700%	9.8124%	0.00555
5.8201%	0.0155%	1.8244%	0.02954	29.3348%	0.0705%	9.8856%	0.00551
6.0134%	0.0160%	1.8977%	0.02841	29.5709%	0.0710%	9.9589%	0.00547
6.2070%	0.0165%	1.9710%	0.02737	29.8074%	0.0715%	10.0322%	0.00543
6.4010%	0.0170%	2.0443%	0.02640	30.0444%	0.0720%	10.1055%	0.00539
6.5953%	0.0175%	2.1175%	0.02549	30.2817%	0.0725%	10.1788%	0.00535
6.7900%	0.0180%	2.1908%	0.02465	30.5195%	0.0730%	10.2521%	0.00531
6.9850%	0.0185%	2.2641%	0.02386	30.7578%	0.0735%	10.3253%	0.00527
7.1804%	0.0190%	2.3374%	0.02312	30.9965%	0.0740%	10.3986%	0.00524
7.3762%	0.0195%	2.4107%	0.02242	31.2356%	0.0745%	10.4719%	0.00520
7.5723%	0.0200%	2.4840%	0.02177	31.4751%	0.0750%	10.5452%	0.00517

7.7687%	0.0205%	2.5572%	0.02115	31.7151%	0.0755%	10.6185%	0.00513
7.9655%	0.0210%	2.6305%	0.02057	31.9555%	0.0760%	10.6918%	0.00509
8.1627%	0.0215%	2.7038%	0.02001	32.1964%	0.0765%	10.7650%	0.00506
8.3603%	0.0220%	2.7771%	0.01949	32.4377%	0.0770%	10.8383%	0.00503
8.5581%	0.0225%	2.8504%	0.01899	32.6794%	0.0775%	10.9116%	0.00499
8.7564%	0.0230%	2.9237%	0.01852	32.9216%	0.0780%	10.9849%	0.00496
8.9550%	0.0235%	2.9969%	0.01807	33.1642%	0.0785%	11.0582%	0.00493
9.1540%	0.0240%	3.0702%	0.01764	33.4072%	0.0790%	11.1315%	0.00489
9.3533%	0.0245%	3.1435%	0.01724	33.6507%	0.0795%	11.2048%	0.00486
9.5530%	0.0250%	3.2168%	0.01685	33.8947%	0.0800%	11.2780%	0.00483
9.7531%	0.0255%	3.2901%	0.01647	34.1391%	0.0805%	11.3513%	0.00480
9.9535%	0.0260%	3.3634%	0.01612	34.3839%	0.0810%	11.4246%	0.00477
10.1543%	0.0265%	3.4367%	0.01578	34.6292%	0.0815%	11.4979%	0.00474
10.3555%	0.0270%	3.5099%	0.01545	34.8749%	0.0820%	11.5712%	0.00471
10.5570%	0.0275%	3.5832%	0.01513	35.1210%	0.0825%	11.6445%	0.00468
10.7589%	0.0280%	3.6565%	0.01483	35.3677%	0.0830%	11.7177%	0.00465
10.9612%	0.0285%	3.7298%	0.01454	35.6147%	0.0835%	11.7910%	0.00462
11.1638%	0.0290%	3.8031%	0.01426	35.8622%	0.0840%	11.8643%	0.00459
11.3668%	0.0295%	3.8764%	0.01400	36.1102%	0.0845%	11.9376%	0.00456
11.5702%	0.0300%	3.9496%	0.01374	36.3586%	0.0850%	12.0109%	0.00454
11.7739%	0.0305%	4.0229%	0.01349	36.6075%	0.0855%	12.0842%	0.00451
11.9780%	0.0310%	4.0962%	0.01325	36.8568%	0.0860%	12.1574%	0.00448
12.1825%	0.0315%	4.1695%	0.01302	37.1066%	0.0865%	12.2307%	0.00445
12.3874%	0.0320%	4.2428%	0.01279	37.3568%	0.0870%	12.3040%	0.00443
12.5926%	0.0325%	4.3161%	0.01258	37.6075%	0.0875%	12.3773%	0.00440
12.7982%	0.0330%	4.3893%	0.01237	37.8587%	0.0880%	12.4506%	0.00438
13.0042%	0.0335%	4.4626%	0.01217	38.1103%	0.0885%	12.5239%	0.00435
13.2105%	0.0340%	4.5359%	0.01197	38.3623%	0.0890%	12.5971%	0.00433
13.4172%	0.0345%	4.6092%	0.01178	38.6148%	0.0895%	12.6704%	0.00430
13.6244%	0.0350%	4.6825%	0.01160	38.8678%	0.0900%	12.7437%	0.00428
13.8318%	0.0355%	4.7558%	0.01142	39.1212%	0.0905%	12.8170%	0.00425
14.0397%	0.0360%	4.8290%	0.01125	39.3751%	0.0910%	12.8903%	0.00423
14.2479%	0.0365%	4.9023%	0.01108	39.6295%	0.0915%	12.9636%	0.00420
14.4565%	0.0370%	4.9756%	0.01092	39.8843%	0.0920%	13.0369%	0.00418
14.6655%	0.0375%	5.0489%	0.01076	40.1396%	0.0925%	13.1101%	0.00416
14.8749%	0.0380%	5.1222%	0.01061	40.3954%	0.0930%	13.1834%	0.00413

15.0847%	0.0385%	5.1955%	0.01046	40.6516%	0.0935%	13.2567%	0.00411
15.2948%	0.0390%	5.2688%	0.01031	40.9083%	0.0940%	13.3300%	0.00409
15.5053%	0.0395%	5.3420%	0.01017	41.1654%	0.0945%	13.4033%	0.00407
15.7162%	0.0400%	5.4153%	0.01004	41.4230%	0.0950%	13.4766%	0.00404
15.9275%	0.0405%	5.4886%	0.00990	41.6811%	0.0955%	13.5498%	0.00402
16.1392%	0.0410%	5.5619%	0.00977	41.9397%	0.0960%	13.6231%	0.00400
16.3513%	0.0415%	5.6352%	0.00965	42.1987%	0.0965%	13.6964%	0.00398
16.5637%	0.0420%	5.7085%	0.00952	42.4582%	0.0970%	13.7697%	0.00396
16.7765%	0.0425%	5.7817%	0.00940	42.7182%	0.0975%	13.8430%	0.00394
16.9898%	0.0430%	5.8550%	0.00929	42.9786%	0.0980%	13.9163%	0.00392
17.2034%	0.0435%	5.9283%	0.00917	43.2395%	0.0985%	13.9895%	0.00390
17.4174%	0.0440%	6.0016%	0.00906	43.5009%	0.0990%	14.0628%	0.00388
17.6318%	0.0445%	6.0749%	0.00895	43.7628%	0.0995%	14.1361%	0.00386
17.8465%	0.0450%	6.1482%	0.00884	44.0251%	0.1000%	14.2094%	0.00384
18.0617%	0.0455%	6.2214%	0.00874	44.2880%	0.1005%	14.2827%	0.00382
18.2773%	0.0460%	6.2947%	0.00864	44.5513%	0.1010%	14.3560%	0.00380
18.4932%	0.0465%	6.3680%	0.00854	44.8150%	0.1015%	14.4292%	0.00378
18.7096%	0.0470%	6.4413%	0.00844	45.0793%	0.1020%	14.5025%	0.00376
18.9263%	0.0475%	6.5146%	0.00835	45.3440%	0.1025%	14.5758%	0.00374
19.1434%	0.0480%	6.5879%	0.00826	45.6093%	0.1030%	14.6491%	0.00372
19.3610%	0.0485%	6.6611%	0.00817	45.8750%	0.1035%	14.7224%	0.00370
19.5789%	0.0490%	6.7344%	0.00808	46.1411%	0.1040%	14.7957%	0.00368
19.7972%	0.0495%	6.8077%	0.00799	46.4078%	0.1045%	14.8689%	0.00367
20.0159%	0.0500%	6.8810%	0.00791	46.6750%	0.1050%	14.9422%	0.00365
20.2351%	0.0505%	6.9543%	0.00782	46.9426%	0.1055%	15.0155%	0.00363
20.4546%	0.0510%	7.0276%	0.00774	47.2108%	0.1060%	15.0888%	0.00361
20.6745%	0.0515%	7.1008%	0.00766	47.4794%	0.1065%	15.1621%	0.00359
20.8948%	0.0520%	7.1741%	0.00758	47.7485%	0.1070%	15.2354%	0.00358
21.1155%	0.0525%	7.2474%	0.00751	48.0181%	0.1075%	15.3087%	0.00356
21.3367%	0.0530%	7.3207%	0.00743	48.2882%	0.1080%	15.3819%	0.00354
21.5582%	0.0535%	7.3940%	0.00736	48.5587%	0.1085%	15.4552%	0.00353
21.7801%	0.0540%	7.4673%	0.00729	48.8298%	0.1090%	15.5285%	0.00351
22.0024%	0.0545%	7.5406%	0.00722	49.1014%	0.1095%	15.6018%	0.00349
22.2252%	0.0550%	7.6138%	0.00715	49.3734%	0.1100%	15.6751%	0.00348
22.4483%	0.0555%	7.6871%	0.00708	49.6460%	0.1105%	15.7484%	0.00346
22.6719%	0.0560%	7.7604%	0.00701	49.9191%	0.1110%	15.8216%	0.00345

22.8958%	0.0565%	7.8337%	0.00695	50.1926%	0.1115%	15.8949%	0.00343
23.1202%	0.0570%	7.9070%	0.00688	50.4666%	0.1120%	15.9682%	0.00341
23.3449%	0.0575%	7.9803%	0.00682	50.7412%	0.1125%	16.0415%	0.00340
23.5701%	0.0580%	8.0535%	0.00676	51.0162%	0.1130%	16.1148%	0.00338

Baroque Omaha: How should I use this table? I only see lists of data but can you provide some examples to show how the table works?

Professor Dong: Yes. Column A presents the expected annual return, and it is the goal return that your demand dictates. Column B translates into your daily return. Column C is the most optimal loss level that you might incur at 1% probability per day. Column D is a benchmark that you use to compare your stock to, so that you can tell what its possible return and risk will be.

For example, the first group of shaded data reads:

5.0506%	0.0135%	1.5313%	0.03511

This means that if you want to get a return of 5.0506% per year, you need to be prepared for a daily loss of at least 1.5313%. The likelihood of realizing such a loss is 1%.

So, you can apply the interpretation to all of the data listed in the table. For example, the second group of shaded data reads:

10.1543%	0.0265%	3.4367%	0.01578

This means that if you want to get a return of 10.1543% per year from one stock, you have 1% chance every day of incurring a loss of 3.4367% or more than that.

Please use caution when applying this table to your investment decisions. This table assumes that there is a normal distribution of asset return, which might not be the case in the real world.

Moselle Omaha: But if I lose 3.4367% or more in a day, all my investment capital would be gone in about 30 days. How can I make an annual return of 10.1543%?

Professor Dong: Such reasoning is actually incorrect. The loss rate of 3.4367% has a 1% chance of becoming true every day. In other words, every day you have a 99% likelihood of receiving a return better than a loss of 3.4367%. In addition, incurring a 3.4367% loss in a day does not mean you will necessarily incur that again and again in the next 29 days. Worst case scenario, if you had really bad luck one day and the 1% probability were to be realized, the next day you would have, again, a 99% chance of receiving a return better than -3.4367%.

As a matter of fact, the likelihood of realizing the continuous 1% chance of incurring loss all 30 days and end up losing all of your investment capital is

$$1\%^{30}=0.000000000000000000000000000000000000000000000000000000000001$$

Wanna Buffet: That's much better. What is the risk-return reward relationship in column D? And how do I use it?

Professor Dong: That is the essence of the table and also the reason you should dog-ear the page so you can check back often.

To use it, you first need to know how to calculate the standard deviation of the return of a stock.

Please go to Yahoo! Finance and download the historical price of a stock. Here, I am using Nike (NYSE: NKE) as an example. Key the ticker "NKE" into the box as shown below and click on "Go".

Now click on "Historical Prices" as shown below:

Please fill in the time period of data, select "daily", and click on "get prices." The time period should consist of the most recent 10 years. I recommend you contact me to obtain the most recent risk-return reward table. If you do not have the most recent table provided by me, you should be consistent with the risk-return reward table by using the period of February 14, 2006 to February 14, 2016. If your stock does not have such a long history, just use the Yahoo! Finance default setting and obtain the longest possible period available. Please see the following figure.

Now scroll to the bottom of the page and right click the "Download to Spreadsheet" link to save the file. See the following figure.

Open the price file you have just downloaded in Excel. Double-click the cell H2. Then, in cell H2, enter =G2/G3-1, as shown in the following figure. Press enter. You have now successfully computed the stock's return from its daily price. However, this is only one return for one recent transaction. We also need to compute all the returns beyond this.

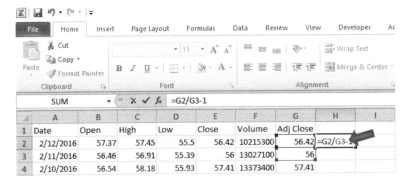

Click on cell H2 again and move the cursor to the lower right portion of the cell until the cursor becomes a solid black plus sign. Double click so that the formula is expanded to all of column H. Please see the following figure.

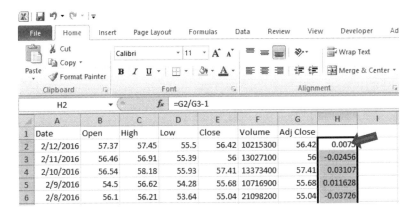

Go to the bottom of the spreadsheet, and delete the cell that shows "#DIV/0!" as you can see in the image below.

8873	12/10/1980	9.87456	9.87456	9.50016	9.50016	5875200	0.114955	-0.06175
8874	12/9/1980	10.37504	10.37504	10.12544	10.12544	5824000	0.122521	-0.02406
8875	12/8/1980	10.49984	10.49984	10.37504	10.37504	5414400	0.125541	-0.05684
8876	12/5/1980	11.24992	11.24992	11.00032	11.00032	7590400	0.133107	-0.05373
8877	12/4/1980	11.62496	11.7504	11.62496	11.62496	22694400	0.140665	0.033337
8878	12/3/1980	11.37536	11.37536	11.24992	11.24992	25177600	0.136127	-0.02176
8879	12/2/1980	11.50016	11.7504	11.50016	11.50016	1.01E+08	0.139155	#DIV/0!
8880								
8881								

In any blank cell, key in =stdev.s(h:h) as is demonstrated in the following figure. Press enter.

76

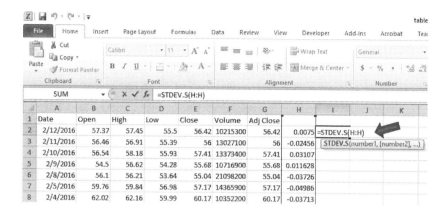

Use 0.000234655786 to divide the output of =stdev.s(h:h) and you will get the risk-return reward relationship of your stock. For example, if the output is 0.01774, then your stock's risk-return reward is:

$$0.000234655786 \div 0.022076 = 0.013228.$$

Now, go back to the Risk-Return Reward Table and in Column D, look for the reward value closest to 0.013228. Here is what you will find:

2.0277%	0.0055%	0.3587%	0.14272
2.2141%	0.0060%	0.4320%	0.11977

Since 0.013228 is between the two risk-return reward values, 0.14272 and 0.11977, you can now conclude that this stock would very likely generate on average an annual return of approximately 2.1% and that its risk is that every day you will have a 1% chance of incurring a loss of 0.38% or more.

Baroque Omaha: Wow! That's very impressive. But it's also a long process. Can you give us some cookbook guidelines?

Professor Dong: Yes! In a nutshell, you need to keep in mind the following steps:

1. Go to Yahoo! Finance and download the stock price.

2. Use the adjusted close price to compute the return, the "=g2/g3-1" step.

3. Delete the last invalid return and compute the standard deviation, the "DIV/0!" step and the "=stdev.s(h:h)" step.

4. Divide 0.000234655786 by the =stdev.s(h:h) output and compare the result with the Risk-Return Reward Table, Column D.

5. Conclude the stock's average expected return and its risk.

7 INVESTMENT STRATEGIES

Stilleven Jobs: What do you mean by "investment strategy"?

Professor Dong: It refers to the planning and functionality of a portfolio. It involves making key decisions related to your investment's performance.

In this chapter, I will discuss the following key decisions: making passive or active investments; buying large or small stocks; buying high or low dividend stocks; buying high or low liquidity stocks; making a long or short term investment.

In the future chapters and volumes, I will continue to discuss the following key decisions related to investment strategy: risk hedging, portfolio rebalancing, industrial weight, and dynamic management. These topics are too big to include in this single chapter.

Moselle Omaha: What is passive management? And, what is active management?

Professor Dong: Passive management describes the style in which investors only invest in ETFs that track broad market indexes, instead of analyzing and investing in individual assets. Passive investment takes into account the broad market performance. For example, a passive investor tracking the U.S. equity market might invest in the long position of DIA (the ETF that tracks the Dow Jones Industrial Average Index), or she might invest in the long position of SPY (the ETF that tracks the Standard and Poor's 500 Index).

In the U.S. equity market, there are three main ETFs that track the broad market indexes: DIA which tracks Dow, SPY which tracks S&P 500, and QQQ which tracks NASDAQ.

Active management, on the other hand, is the style in which investors analyze and invest in individual assets. These investors aim to beat the broad market index by searching for assets that appreciate more when the market also appreciates, yet that depreciate less when the market depreciates. Investors who are doing stock picking analysis and portfolio diversification analysis are regarded as active style investors.

The semi-active strategy is a mix of the passive and active strategies. It means to actively explore ETFs or sector ETFs in accordance with a specific theme. However, at the individual asset level, the semi-active strategy remains passive. In other words, the semi-active strategy entails actively selecting sectors or themes and expecting returns that can beat the broad market index; however, it passively includes all of the representative equities in the sector or theme without selecting among them.

Moselle Omaha: What is the "market cap"? And, what are a small cap stock, a midcap stock, and a large cap stock?

Professor Dong: "Market cap" is the short form of market capitalization. It is the product of the current price of the stock multiplied by its amount of outstanding common shares. Market cap is used to measure a stock's size.

Small Cap, in common market practice is less than a $1 billion market cap. If a stock's market cap is between $1 and $5 billion, it is regarded as a mid-cap. Large cap stocks have market caps greater than $5 billion.

Baroque Omaha: Of small, mid, or large caps, which stock size performs the best in the market?

Professor Dong: To address the question we should actually ask: which size has a higher volatility.

Fama and French (and because of their research, Fama is the Nobel laureate of 2013) found that smaller stocks have higher returns compared to larger stocks when the market is experiencing an upward trend; yet, smaller stocks incur more loss when the market is in a downward trend. Therefore it is not reasonable to conclude that a certain size of stock can promise the most market returns.

Stilleven Jobs: What are growth stocks and value stocks?

Professor Dong: Growth stocks have higher Price/Earnings ratio, Price/Book ratio, Price/Sales ratio, and Price/Cash Flow ratios. Those ratios for value stocks are lower. Value stocks tend to pay a significant amount of dividends or enforce certain types of share repurchase programs. Yet, growth stocks tend to reserve cash for business expansion.

Growth companies usually carry higher stock prices. These companies are believed to have "good stories" which indicate a trend toward future capital appreciation. These stocks do not typically pay high dividends or apply share repurchases. Such companies hold cash and aggressively invest in future opportunities. Typically, there are more growth-type firms from the technology sector, the telecommunication sector, and from biological-product related firms. These firms are expected to double or even triple their stock prices when a certain event or outcome is reached, such as if a new drug is approved by the FDA, or a new technology is protected by an approved patent.

Value companies usually carry lower stock prices. These companies, called "cash cows," do not have "good stories" but have mature statuses and have established market share. The value stocks do not appreciate significantly because of the limit of market capacity. However, these companies pay a decent amount of dividends or perform share repurchases because they lack investment opportunities. The names of value firms are usually well recognized and are regarded as industry leaders. Typically, there are more value-type firms from the utility sector, the energy sector, and from financial service-related firms.

Moselle Omaha: Which type of stock performs better in the equity market?

Professor Dong: To answer this question, I would like to cite the research conducted by the Fidelity Fund. You can retrieve the full article called value investing vs growth investing from the learning center of their website: fidelity.com.

"[The] annualized return of growth-oriented large-cap U.S. stock was 9.91 percent (which represents the average of the Dow Jones Large Cap Growth Index and the Dow Jones U.S. Large Cap Growth Index).

Large-cap U.S. stock with a value orientation had a higher average return than large-cap U.S. stock with a growth orientation. This difference in favor of value is referred to as a value premium.

The average annualized return of two midcap value indexes (Dow Jones Mid Cap Value and Dow Jones U.S. Mid Cap Value) was 13.51 percent, considerably better than the 11.27 percent average return of the combined midcap growth indexes.

Among small-cap U.S. equity indexes, the value premium was an astonishing 420 basis points (bps); that is, a value return of 14.13 percent minus a growth return of 9.93 percent equals a value premium of 420 bps. With an annualized return of 14.13 percent, small-cap value turned $10,000 into $601,860, or $413,753 more than the ending balance in small-cap growth.

Large-cap value demonstrated a performance premium 67 percent of the time. The average five-year value premium was 476 bps. Conversely, large-cap growth outperformed large-cap value 33 percent of the time by an average of 316 bps.

Among midcap equity indexes, value also outperformed growth 67 percent of the time by an average of 575 bps (over five-year periods). When growth outperformed value (33 percent of the time), the margin of victory averaged

284 bps. Among midcap U.S. stocks, a value tilt has historically provided better performance than a growth tilt.

Among small-cap U.S. equity indexes, value beat growth 70 percent of the time by an average of 756 basis points (again, over five-year periods). However, when small-cap growth outperforms (30 percent of the time), the difference can be large. Overall, however, when small growth outperformed small-cap value, the average margin of victory was only 220 bps.

These results do not argue for eliminating growth-oriented assets from a portfolio. However, this analysis does suggest that a value "tilt" may be justified in the long run."

Wanna Buffet: Okay, so what is high dividend stock?

Professor Dong: High dividend stocks pay out high earnings to their shareholders. Please note that the direct comparison of dividend dollar amounts across stocks is not meaningful. For example, if you invest $500 to buy stock ABC at the price of $5 per share, and ABC announces that they will pay a $0.50 dividend per share, you will receive $50 in dividends. Yet if you invest $500 in stock XYZ at the price of $25 per share, and ABC announces that they will pay $1 in dividends per share, you will receive $2 in dividends.

The only meaningful comparison is dividend yield. It is calculated as the dividend per share, divided by the price of the stock per share. In the previous case, the dividend yield of ABC was 10%, which is 0.50/5; the dividend yield of XYZ is 4%, which is 1/25.

Wanna Buffet: This is valuable information! Should I just invest in high dividend stocks and receive the dividends then?

Professor Dong: Well, not necessarily. Please keep in mind that the day the firm records the dividend payment, the stock price will drop by approximately the same amount as the dividend. So it is not necessarily true that if you buy a stock that pays an annual dividend of 28% that you will realize a total return of 28% per year.

Wanna Buffet: So can I receive the dividend and sell the stock before the price drops? How do I harvest dividend?

Professor Dong: Unfortunately, that is not possible. I would like to cite a very precise and well-organized article from Daniela Pylypczak. It is titled *everything investors need to know about ex-dividend dates* and can be retrieved from the dividend education sites at dividend.com.

According to Pylypczak, there are four days that are related to the dividend payment: the declaration day, the ex-dividend day, the record day, and the day of payment. The ex-dividend day is the most important and the most relevant to investors. Pylypczak writes:

"The declaration date is the day that the company declares that it will pay a dividend. With this declaration, the company announces how much it will pay, the ex-dividend date, and the payment date. The declaration date is sometimes called the 'announcement date' and most reliable dividend-paying companies keep to a regular declaration schedule (adjusting for weekends and holidays, of course)…"

"As for the ex-dividend date, buyers of this stock will no longer be entitled to receive the declared dividend and the stock is said to thereafter trade 'ex-dividend' (without dividend). Before trading opens on the ex-dividend date, the exchange marks down the share price by the amount of the declared dividend. As an example, ABC Inc. declares a $1 dividend with an ex-dividend date of January 10th. Anybody who buys the shares on the 7th, 8th, or 9th—or any date prior to the 10th—will get that dividend. When the stock opens on the 10th, it will be adjusted down by $1 from the 9th's closing price. Anybody who buys on the 10th or thereafter will not get the dividend."

"Another important note to consider: as long as you purchase a stock prior to the ex-dividend date, you can then sell the stock any time on or after the ex-dividend date and still receive the dividend. A common misconception is that investors need to hold the stock through the record date or pay date. "

"The record date is simply the date where the company looks at its ledger and determines to whom they send the dividend checks ('the holders of record'). The record date is always two business days after the ex-dividend date (business days being non-holidays and non-weekends). This date is completely inconsequential for dividend investors, since eligibility is determined solely by the ex-dividend date."

"The payment date (or 'pay date') is the date on which a company actually pays out its dividend. Generally speaking, this date falls about two weeks to one month after the ex-dividend date."

Baroque Omaha: What role does dividend play in terms of strategizing my investment portfolio?

Professor Dong: Dividend stocks are usually issued more matured value companies. While dividend payment reduces the stock price, it allows cash flow to be delivered to investors sooner and in a more disciplined way. Firms that start to pay dividend seldom reduce the dividend payment unless they experience financial stress and borrowing money in order to pay the dividend is not an available option during the stress.

Therefore, stocks from high dividend companies can serve as good hedging tools to protect against the potential risk of a portfolio. While these firms pay out some of their earnings per share and this might sacrifice some reinvestment opportunities, such a portion being paid out can be reinvested by investors at their discretion.

Moselle Omaha: What is high liquidity stock and what are its features?

Professor Dong: In academia, liquidity is defined as the degree of price discount or premium offered to reach a quick, bulk transaction.

Stocks that are highly liquid have many floating shares in the market place. Thus it is easier to purchase them without waiting long or triggering a large price increase; even the amount of shares being purchased is huge. Stocks that are highly liquid are also easier to borrow and sell short. Liquid stocks have, on average, higher daily trading volumes, and investors can see continuous price charts for those stocks. Illiquid stocks have low daily trading volumes, and the price charts are discrete and have gaps.

The liquidity of stocks can be measured by the bid-ask spread of the transaction. The wider the spread, the more illiquid the asset is. Stocks with low liquidity should generate a higher return to compensate the inconvenience brought about by illiquidity.

Stilleven Jobs: What is long term investment? How about short term investment?

Professor Dong: Long term investment refers to holding the equity for more than one year. Short term investment refers to a holding period of less than one year, and ultra-short term refers to a position that lasts for less than a week.

Historically, long term investments generate significantly better average annual returns than short term investments, for three reasons: first, frequent opening and closing positions generate a large transaction cost, mainly including a bid-ask spread cost and a commission cost; second, frequent operations on positions and investment decisions incur opportunity cost, mainly the cost of failing to trigger a limit order and missing the opportunity of profit; last, there is the potential of making the wrong decision due to a lack of consideration and also because of the psychological limits of human nature, meaning rushing to buy, rushing to close profit, or delaying in lock loss.

Another issue is related to investors who need to file tax reports to the U.S. IRS. This includes U.S. citizens, U.S. permanent residents, and other investors who are obligated.

Short-term capital gains are taxed as ordinary income. This means any income you receive from short term investments will be taxed normally. If your normal income tax bracket is 20%, you would need to pay 20% of the short-term capital gains from investing in stocks.

Long-term capital gains are taxed as pure capital gains and the rate is lower than the ordinary income tax rate, sometimes by 20%.

According to Claire Boyte-White in her famous article *Comparing Long-Term Vs. Short-Term Capital Gain Tax Rates*, "in 2015, the capital gains rate for those in the 10 and 15% income tax brackets is 0%, meaning those who earn the

least are not required to pay any income tax on profits from investments held
longer than one year. For those in the 25 to 35% tax brackets, the capital gains
tax is 15%. For the wealthiest citizens who fall into the 39.6% income tax
bracket, the capital gains rate is still only 20%."

"In general, dividend income is taxed at your ordinary income tax rate.
However, if your investment meets certain requirements, your dividends may
be considered qualified and are subject to the long-term capital gains rate
instead."

8 INVESTMENT TACTICS

Moselle Omaha: What is the difference between an investment strategy, as you were talking about in the previous chapter, and an investment tactic as you talk about in this chapter?

Professor Dong: Investment strategy deals with the question of in which types of stocks should one invest. It focuses on the general investment direction and is a reflection of the investor's investment strategy.

Investment tactic deals with the question of how to select stocks from the pool determined by your investment strategy, and how to implement investing in the stocks selected.

For example, if you have identified in your portfolio that the large cap growth stock should weigh 30%, the large cap value stock should weigh 40%, and the mid cap blend international stock ETF should weigh 30%, these would then fall into the investment strategy scale. Then, investment tactics will deal with searching the best stocks or ETFs in each portion of the portfolio, as well as with how to invest, *i.e.*, when you should open a position, and when you should close it.

Baroque Omaha: How should we understand investment tactics? Can you introduce the structure first?

Professor Dong: Sure! We divide the tactics into two types: for the long term investment strategy and for the short term one.

For long term investment strategies, the tactics that matter are long term stock selection criteria. For short and mid-term investment strategies, the relevant tactics are more complicated. Such tactics include event trading, order timing, and short term stock selection.

For both strategies, the tactics that matter are the entry and exit points, as well as the position control.

Moselle Omaha: So can we start with the common tactic. You mentioned that it is the position control?

Professor Dong: Sure. Position control deals with the question of the amount of cash being used for a stock or ETF, as well as the dynamic management of the cash usage.

First let's review sectors and industries. Sectors are broader concepts, such as health care or financials. Industries are the subcategories under sectors, such as the banking industry or insurance industry, which are both under the financial sector umbrella.

You should keep approximately 10-25 stocks in the portfolio from different industries. If two stocks are from the same or closely-related industry, those two are regarded as one stock. For each stock, the weight should not be more than 10% of the total cash in your account under very extreme cases; in usual cases, the weight of a stock should be no more than 5%. For two stocks that are from the same industry, their weights together should be less than 10%.

A rule of thumb in terms of ETFs is that one ETF is regarded as the equivalent of 5 stocks. The weight of an ETF should not be more than 20% of your total cash balance of your account, unless you simply want to track the broad market return. In that case, you might spend 100% of your cash on ETFs such as SPY, which tracks the S&P500 index return, or DIA, which tracks the Dow Jones Industrial Average return.

Stilleven Jobs: Can you give us an example of position control?

Professor Dong: Yes. The following portfolio presents a typical weight allocation in terms of cash investments. The weights in the table are at the maximum permitted level to diversify risk. As the investor has an extremely strong preference for the Apple stock, its weight goes to 10%. Normally, 5% is the cap for a single stock investment position.

The portfolio is well-diversified. As I mentioned earlier, stocks from the same industry are regarded as one stock. So there are six single stocks in this portfolio, counting CVX and XOM as one. As there are three ETFs in the portfolio and none of the components repeat the individual stocks held, the portfolio is regarded as the equivalent of having 21 stock holdings.

			Portfolio	
Asset Ticker	Asset Name	Asset Type	Asset's Industry	Asset Weight
AAPL	Apple	Common Stock	Technology	10%
BA	Boeing	Common	Industrial	5%

		Stock		
CVX	Chevron	Common Stock	Crude Oil Energy	5%
XOM	Exxon Mobile	Common Stock	Crude Oil Energy	5%
GS	Goldman Sachs	Common Stock	Financials	5%
HD	Home Depot	Common Stock	Retail	5%
UNH	United Health	Common Stock	Health Care	5%
IEUS	European Small Cap	ETF	All industries in developed EU markets	20%
VWO	Emerging Market	ETF	All industries in U.S. consumer staples sector	20%
VDC	U.S. Consumer Staples stocks	ETF	All industries in developing countries	20%

Wanna Buffet: Can you introduce the entry point tactic?

Professor Dong: Yes. This is also a common tactic that both short and long term investment strategies focus on. There is no perfect answer for the single best entry point tactic. Yet, my answer can give you some common clues and reasoning on the issue of deciding which entry point is for you.

For short term investment with an investment horizon of less than one year, the entry point is a very sensitive topic. An unfortunate entry point can turn a correct strategy into a loss. Think about the following scenario. After an extensive analysis, you determine that a company has very good potential, and you purchased its stock, planning to sell it within one year to pay off your student loan. However, other investors have made the same judgment as yours and they have taken action earlier than you. So while the company might be a good one, its current price is too high to be justified.

Investors always want to make a good profit deal in the investments. In a nutshell, the goal is to buy low and sell high for long positions, and to sell high and buy back low for short positions.

However, this involves two concerns: Are you buying low (will the price drop after you purchase)? And, are you selling high (will the price increases after you sell)?

Sadly, the answers to those questions are: we can never guarantee an ideal low purchase or high sell. As we previously mentioned, market price at a day-to-day basis is stochastic.

This does not mean that there is no clue at all. Stock prices can be low due to four reasons:

Reason 1: A one-time negative event within the firm that does not involve any lasting damage to the firm's performance.

Example: News about the firm's parking lot catching fire, resulting in the death of two people.
Example: News about a labor union's strike causing pause on a shipment of goods.

Reason 2: Negative events within the firm that involve lasting damage to the firm's performance.

Example: News that the firm's new drug was not approved by FDA.
Example: News that the firm has quit the Latin American market and has a low quarterly earnings report.

Reason 3: A one-time negative event of capital market that does not involve any lasting damage to the macro-economy or the industry in which the firm operates.

Example: News about market disappointed at the presidential candidate's performance.
Example: News about increasing tension between N. Korea and the U.S.

Reason 4: negative events of capital market that involve lasting damage to the macro-economy or the industry in which the firm operates.

Example: News that the federal reserve has determined to increase its interest rate.
Example: News about increasing regulations on the environmental impact of the product in an industry.

In short, if the stock price is low because of reasons one or three, the stock price is not likely to be continuously low or even greatly lower. So the low price of a stock caused by reason one or three in fact makes for a good entry point. Yet, for low stock prices because of reasons two or four, it is recommended to avoid the stock.

Moselle Omaha: Can we conclude that the exit point follows a similar logic?

Professor Dong: Roughly speaking, yes. However, the point of selling is more complicated. You do not have an obligation to buy an asset. So you buy simply because you want to buy it.

However, after you have purchased it, you have the obligation of selling it. This is because all you want is the return from the asset, rather than the asset itself. In other words, you are obligated to convert the asset back into liquid purchasing power sooner or later. Therefore, when you sell an asset, it may be because you *want* to sell it, yet sometimes it is because you *have* to sell it, no matter it is because of the problem of the position, or it is due to your other needs.

The reason you want to sell an asset, whether it is something that you have purchased previously or you are simply selling short without holding, is because you believe the price is good enough. Usually five categories of factors can lead to such a belief:

Reason 1: A one-time positive event within the firm that is not a persistent driving force for the firm's performance in the long run. You thus believe that in the long run the firm would not deliver a performance that meets your expectation.

Example: A piece of one-time negative news about the firm's competitor.

Reason 2: A one-time positive event in the general capital market that is not a persistent driving force for the firm's performance in the long run. You thus believe that in the long run the firm would not deliver a performance that meets your expectation.

Example: The U. S. Department of Labor published new nonfarm payroll data that is beyond the analysts' expectation. The U.S. stock market closed 3% higher. A stock whose major business is in Asia also increases by 2.5%.

Reason 3: The price of the asset has realized continuous increases and you do not think such a trend is sustainable.

Example: A stock has maintained five positive returns in a row, and its holder is worried that the price is too high and investors might be irrational.

Reason 4: The performance of the asset has reached or outperformed the mental goal you set up.

Example: When you invested in a stock, you might assign it a target price, or assign this investment a target return. Once the target is reached, you decide the asset "has fulfilled its mission and should retire".

Reason 5: The investor wants to realize the loss from investing in the asset and receive tax credit.

Example: Investors usually sell assets that are in red to generate tax credit on investment loss. This becomes very popular around the end of the tax year.

You usually have to sell an asset for one of these reasons:

Reason 6: The asset has incurred loss and it is likely going to bring further loss.

Example: Investors are usually reluctant to sell assets that are incurring loss. But, stopping the loss in a timely manner can avoid massive loss and also reserve the cash flow for future investment opportunities.

Reason 7: You are facing a liquidity constraint and you need to pull money out of the account.

Example: The down payment of a house mortgage, a sudden health issue of a family member, and your education or your kids' can all create such a demand.

Reason 8: The performance of the asset is disappointing, and you have identified a new asset investment opportunity so you would like to switch your holding.

Example: Hypothetically, you have been holding XYZ for 4 months and the cumulative return is 0.3%. Through your analysis you find that stock ABC might have good appreciation potential. So you plan to release your cash by selling XYZ and investing in ABC.

Reason 9: The risk of this asset mismatches with other assets in the portfolio.

Example: Hypothetically, after a long period of growth, the weight of AT&T in your portfolio is large, and you also have other risk exposure in the portfolio from the same industry. You are considering shrinking the risk exposure to this single industry by reducing the holding on AT&T.

Baroque Omaha: Wow, these make sense. I really do consider selling a stock in real practice due to one of those nine reasons.

Professor Dong: Keep in mind that though these nine reasons are the ones that drive investors to sell an asset, it does not mean they are all justified. Here are some instances that *should* trigger a sale:

Reason 1: There is a one-time positive event for the firm, yet the firm's long-term perspective is not bright.

Decision: It is a good point to sell.

Reason 2: There is a one-time positive event in the general capital market, yet the firm's long term perspective is not bright.

Decision: It is a good point to sell.

Reason 3: The price of the asset has realized continuous increases.

Decision: You need to use great caution. Price movement always has a reason, though you might not know the reason. If the continuous increases of the asset price are because of improving fundamental aspects in the firm, then it is not a good idea to sell. If it is because of market irrationality, selling the asset might be justified. Overall, the chance of price increase is still 50% after continuous increases, according to the empirical research presented earlier.

Investors should avoid the human psychological mindset that "everything will be mean-reverting and price cannot go up forever. Sooner or later it will go down." The problem of such a mindset is that yes, price might be mean-reverting, but the mean remains undefined. If the mean price of an asset is increasing, then some recent price increases do not necessarily imply an upcoming price decrease.

Reason 4: The performance of the asset has reached the mental goal.

Decision: Unless such a mental goal is related to your short term liquidity need, a mental goal should not be the basis of a selling decision. Once again, price movements always have some intrinsic reason. Selling a stock that has appreciated by 10% is like giving up a hen that has proved to be able to lay golden eggs. The question you should ask yourself is: do I still want to buy the asset after I sell it because it hits my goal? If you still regard it as a good asset, selling it might not be a good idea.

Reason 5: You want to harvest loss for tax credit.

Decision: It is a good point to sell.

Reason 6: You want to stop loss.

Decision: Yes, you should sell. However, it is usually the case that some irrational or regulation-forced panic sales trigger your threshold of wanting to stop loss. If you choose to realize the loss at the peak of market pessimistic mode, the loss could be sizable. Experienced traders choose to wait for an adjustment that is caused when the investors in the market who are selling close their positions, and then they execute the stop loss.

Reason 7: Liquidity constraint.

Decision: You should plan the portfolio in advance to avoid such passive liquidation.

Reason 8: To witch assets for the purposes of return.

Decision: After considering transaction cost, selling the asset might be reasonable. Yet investors need to conquer their own mindset of "the stuff I do not have is better," or in other words, "The grass is greener on the other side."

Reason 9: Unreasonable risk of the asset.

Decision: It is a good reason to sell.

Stilleven Jobs: I do not find a reason to sell an asset in your list, which is if the asset has a defect in its fundamental basis. Shouldn't I also sell that type of asset?

Professor Dong: My question to you is: Why did you invested in this asset previously? Before investing in stocks or ETF, you should have done a thorough investigation of its fundamental basis, and an asset with defect should not be considered by you. The only component that is beyond your control is the upcoming unforeseeable changes that dim the future of the company. Needless to say, you should sell the asset.

Baroque Omaha: Makes sense. What is an adding position? How do I add a position?

Professor Dong: Adding position means you spend more cash and invest further into an asset in which you have already invested and with which you are currently holding a position. There are four scenarios in which you should add more positions on an asset:

Scenario 1: In a long term investment, add position to a current position that is running a gain.

Scenario 2: In a long term investment, add position to a current position that is incurring a loss.

Scenario 3: In a short term investment, add position to a current position that is running a gain.

Scenario 4: In a short term investment, add position to a current position that is incurring a loss.

Baroque Omaha: Is this adding position tactic justified under each scenario?

Professor Dong: Not for all of them. Please see the analysis below. The scenarios correspond to the table above.

Scenario 1: Adding a position is justified if the fundamental perspectives of the asset match its current high price. While buying the same asset at a higher price later is not psychologically comfortable, it can be correct. The asset simply continues to use its old name but it is not the same asset anymore. If its fundamentals and operations have improved, it deserves a higher purchasing price.

Scenario 2: Adding position is justified if the current low price is not a result of deteriorating fundamental perspectives of the firm, but simply the result of a temporary negative event of the firm or the broad market sentiment. In fact, investment gurus like Warren Buffett regard the low price period of an asset as a good opportunity to acquire a more premium asset.

Yet as mentioned earlier, there are always intrinsic reasons for price movements. If the asset price decreases because of the investor's pessimistic views on it, this might hint to deteriorating fundamentals of the firm that you as an individual investor are not aware of. Unless you are very certain that the short term price decline of the asset is not related to the firm's long run performance or environment, it is recommended that you do not add a position.

Scenario 3: Adding position is justified if the fundamental perspectives of the asset match its current high price. Yet you need to make sure that the high price is sustainable in the short run on your investment horizon.

Scenario 4: This is not recommended, unless you are very certain that the short term price decline of the asset is not related to the firm's performance, and that the price will recover *very* soon. However, this is difficult to predict.

Stilleven Jobs: How about a position reduction?

Professor Dong: There are two practices of position reduction. The first is to close a portion of the open position when the investor realizes gain from the asset, and the second is to close a portion of the open position for the purpose of stopping loss.

The second type is not recommended. If a stop loss is triggered, it should hedge all of the open risk exposure, instead of part of it. The first type, however, might be utilized as a good way to lock the profit and remains open to the possible greater profit at the upside, if the investor is unclear about the future trend.

9 DIVERSIFICATION AND RISK MANAGEMENT

Stilleven Jobs: My understanding is that the purpose of risk management is to diversify the portfolio, and to diversify the portfolio, I need to buy many different stocks. Is this correct?

Professor Dong: Not quite. The essence of risk management's purpose is to make you take the risk that fits you as an investor.

To diversify the portfolio, you might not need to buy many different stocks. Buying many different stocks does not warrant a diversified portfolio, and a diversified portfolio is only one way to manage risk. What's more, it is very often inappropriately used to manage risk.

Stilleven Jobs: I'm confused. So what do you mean by risk management?

Professor Dong: Risk management means to control the risk so that it does not exceed the maximum level that you can afford to have. This goes against the common belief that "risk management is to limit the risk to its minimum level, and the best practice is to eliminate any risk."

All investors understand that risk and return grow proportionally. While higher risk does not necessarily warrant a higher return, lower risk will never bring a higher return. You can regard the risk of a stock as cost and the return of a stock as revenue. In other words, the risk of a stock is the price you pay to purchase a product, and the return of stock is the benefit you receive from the product that you have purchased. Now it is easier to understand in simpler terms: while more expensive products are not necessarily good, cheap items are most definitely not as good.

Therefore, if you would like to receive a return at a certain level, you would have to take the risk that corresponds to that level. In terms of identifying the level of return that you need, please refer to Chapter Six, under the question "How do you calculate annual return rate demand." In terms of the corresponding risk level for the given required return, please also refer to Chapter Six, under the question, "How do you obtain the risk and return relationship?"

The common belief that "investors should never welcome risk and should always reduce the risk of the portfolio, preferably to zero" is very misleading. As a matter of fact, if risk is reduced to zero, the return investors can get is barely equal to the short term U.S. Treasury bill rate. As of March 2016, the annual short term U.S. Treasury bill rate was only 0.2%. *Risk is the source of return.*

In summary, the correct and wise way of viewing risk management is that managing risk means to strive to be at the level that matches exactly the demand of return. Risk should be no more than that. Thus, avoid introducing excessive volatility that the investor cannot take on. Risk should be no less than the level that the investor can take on either to avoid bringing the investor a disappointing return.

Stilleven Jobs: And what do you mean when you say, "To diversity the portfolio, you might not need to buy many different stocks"?

Professor Dong: Buying many different stocks *can* be a method of diversifying a portfolio. However, it is an expensive and somehow outdated way of doing so. Investors usually need to select and purchase many different stocks to assemble a portfolio in which the stocks represent a variety of industries and performances. According to Statman's famous article "How Many Stocks Make a Diversified Portfolio" published in the *Journal of Finance*, investors need 40 stocks to diversify a portfolio. Considering the commissions, the bid-ask spread, and hassles surrounding buying and selling each of the 40 stocks, buying individual stocks to diversify a portfolio is really not an efficient way to reduce risk.

A more efficient method of diversifying a portfolio is to use ETF to diversify risk. As long as an ETF is not tracking any sector or industry index in which the assets co-move significantly, any ETF that includes stocks from various industries and sectors is in fact well-diversified. In addition, mutual funds, close-ended or open-ended, can also do the job of diversifying the portfolio.

In addition, funds, other than those that focus on one industry, are already well-diversified within their holdings. In other words, these funds are close to the optimal ratio of return and risk. While investors might find and pick stocks that can generate higher returns, these stocks are most likely carrying disproportionally high risk.

The next step is to simply diversify the funds in terms of their styles, no matter if it is ETF, or another type of fund. For example:

If an investor purchases U.S. large cap value stock ETF, then it might be good diversification to add the U.S. small cap growth stock ETF.

If an investor purchases U.S. large cap blend stock ETF, then it might be good diversification to add the emerging market small cap blend stock ETF.

Stilleven Jobs: And what do you mean by "buying many different stocks does not warrant a diversified portfolio"?

Professor Dong: If the stocks are from the same industry, they are more likely highly correlated. These stocks cannot help diversify the risk among one another. For example, the following is a representation of the home furnishing stocks in the top 5 market capitalization:

Ticker	Company Name	Market Capitalization as of Feb 26, 2016
LZB	La-Z-Boy Incorporated	$1216868539
HELE	Helen of Troy Limited	$2695120093
TPX	Tempur Sealy International, Inc.	$3663091372
LEG	Leggett & Platt, Incorporated	$6169218489
MHK	Mohawk Industries, Inc.	$13195188106

The following chart is the stock price history in the recent period:

One caveat is that there is another type of diversification failure that is less explicit. Stocks that are from different industries, yet are similar in terms of their financial report structures, can still be highly correlated, because they are affected by common factors. For example, railroads and semiconductor stocks are seemingly less related, yet both industries are capital intensive. The stock prices in those two industries would decrease together sharply if the Federal interest rate would rise.

Stilleven Jobs: And what do you mean by "a diversified portfolio is only one means for managing risk"?

Professor Dong: There are three ways to manage an existing risky position. For example, say you started investing in stocks and you have spent 10% of your cash to purchase an Apple stock (NYSE: AAPL). You are concerned about the volatility and the risk of this holding:

The first way to manage risk is through conventional diversification: buying other stocks that are irrelevant to the current position. Other methods include hedging the risk, and diversifying the investment strategy and implementation.

To hedge the risk, investors can also use options[10] or inverse ETF.

To diversify the investment strategy as well as the implementation, investors can use various investment styles and methods. For example, a quarter of the portfolio can be actively managed, a quarter passively managed; a quarter implemented by automated algorithm-based trading, and the last quarter blended by actively selecting the passive ETFs.

Stilleven Jobs: And what do you mean when you say, "diversifying a portfolio is too often inappropriately used to manage risk"?

Professor Dong: The common belief that one may diversify the risk by adding more holdings from different stocks, or continuously reduce the portfolio risk is incorrect. Adding more holdings can increase the transaction cost significantly, yet it does not guarantee a lower risk level.

In addition, continuously reducing the portfolio risk might not help in reaching the designated risk goal. When the risk is effectively reduced, the return of the portfolio is decayed.

Moselle Omaha: Can you explain more specifically how to use inverse ETFs to hedge risk?

Professor Dong: The tickers for the most popular inverse ETFs are SH, SDS, SPXU, and SPXS. In addition, VXX can also serve as an inverse ETF.

SH is the inverse of SPY. SPY is the ETF that tracks the Standard and Poor's 500 index. The return of SH is the opposite of SPY. If SPY realizes a return of 3% on a certain day, the return of SH is then -3%. On the other hand, if the return of SPY on a certain day is -5%, the return of SH is 5%.

SDS is two times the inverse of SPY. If SPY realizes a return of 3% on a certain day, the return of SDS is then -6%. On the other hand, if the return of SPY on a certain day is -5%, the return of SH is 10%.

SPXU or SPXS is three times the inverse of SPY. If SPY realizes a return of 3% on a certain day, the return of SPXU or SPXS is then -9%. On the

---

[10] Options are introduced in the next chapter.

other hand, if the return of SPY on a certain day is -5%, the return of SPXU or SPXS is 15%.

Including VXX in the portfolio can also hedge the risk, yet at the expense of sacrificing some benefit. VXX is the ticker of an ETF that tracks the VIX index. VIX is a volatility index that increases when the market is pessimistic and decreases when the market prices of stocks increase.

10 OPTIONS AND ALTERNATIVE STRATEGIES

Moselle Omaha: Can you introduce more specifically some options one can use to hedge the risk?

Professor Dong: There are many investing options to hedge risk. Roughly speaking, you can approach investing with: a single option combining with its corresponding stock to hedge the risk; a combination of multiple options combining with their corresponding stock to hedge the risk; a single option investment to gain exposure to return and risk; or a combination of multiple options to gain exposure to return and risk.

Moselle Omaha: Can you start by first explaining what an option is?

Professor Dong: Sure. An option is an asset granting its holder to buy or sell its corresponding underlying asset at a pre-determined price. There are mainly two types: call options and put options.

A call option is an asset that, once you have purchased it, provides you the privilege to purchase its corresponding underlying asset at the pre-determined price in the future. Yet you do not have any obligation to exercise this privilege.

For example, you spend $2 to purchase an American call option on March 1, 2016. The option corresponds to the American Express stock (NYSE: AXP). The exercise price (also called strike price) is $60 and it expires on January 20, 2017.

This means that on or before January 20, 2017, you can purchase one share of AXP at the price of $60 per share. If it is a European option, then you only have the right to purchase one share of AXP at the price of $60 per share on January 20, 2017, and no sooner.

So on January 20, 2017, if the price of the AXP stock is higher than $60, you would want to exercise your call option and purchase the stock at the exercise price of $60.

Baroque Omaha: Why would I want to buy it at $60? I do not plan to hold the AXP stock.

Professor Dong: If you do not plan to hold it, you should still exercise the call option and buy the stock at $60. Recall that right now the stock price is higher than $60 in the market. After you buy the stock, you can immediately sell the stock at the market price and collect the price difference as profit.

In real world option investments, if you do not wish to hold the underlying asset, you can simply sell the option at a higher price and realize the profit. Your purpose of holding the asset is to sell it sometime later and realize a profit, rather than simply holding the asset because it offers other types of satisfaction beyond the profit. With a higher underlying asset price, in this case the stock price, the option would be more expensive because of the higher gain potential.

Wanna Buffet: What if on January 20, 2017, the stock price is lower than $60?

Professor Dong: Then you simply do not exercise your call option and let it expire. In this case, you lose your initial cost of buying the call option, which is $2.

Wanna Buffet: What if on January 20, 2017, the stock price is between $60 and $62?

Professor Dong: Good question. You would still want to exercise your option. For example, say that on January 20, 2017, the stock price is $60.80—if you exercise the option by buying the stock at $60, and then immediately sell it at $60.80, you make $0.80 profit.

This helps reduce your cost of buying the call option to just $1.20. If you do not exercise your call option, your loss would be $2—the entire cost of buying the call option.

Stilleven Jobs: So buying a call option is like buying insurance?

Professor Dong: Well, yes and no. Yes, in the sense that a call option could secure your loss of investing in an asset at no more than the cost of the call option; no, in the sense that typically insurance will bring a significant payoff when things go bad, yet call options do not bring such a payoff.

In fact, we will see in a while that put options are indeed like insurance. Buying a call option is like buying a coupon.

Usually we obtain coupons for free. Call options are like coupons you

need to pay to own. The price presented on the coupon is similar to the
exercise price of the call option. When you hold the coupon, you can decide
whether you would like to use it during your purchase.

First, you would check the regular price without the discount from the
coupon. If the regular price is even lower or the same as the price with the
coupon, the holder of the coupon should simply discard it. You would use the
coupon if and only if it can help you save some money.

Baroque Omaha: Can you give us a real example of a call option?

Professor Dong: Yes, the price of the common stock Pfizer (NYSE: PFE) as
of March 4, 2016, 4:00pm EST was $29.71. Some of its corresponding call
and put option prices are listed in the table below.

Call option bid price	Call option ask price	Exercise Price	Put option bid price	Put option ask price
		Expires on March 18, 2016		
0.84	0.95	29	0.16	0.18
0.49	0.56	29.5	0.29	0.34
0.26	0.29	30	0.52	0.58
0.09	0.13	30.5	0.86	0.94
		Expires on December 16, 2016		
5.00	5.30	25	0.85	0.90
3.40	4.05	27	1.38	1.43
1.78	1.84	30	2.66	2.73
1.00	1.06	32	3.90	4.00
		Expires on January 19, 2018		
5.50	5.75	25	1.97	2.05
3.60	3.80	28	3.15	3.35
2.62	2.76	30	4.15	4.35
1.85	1.97	32	5.35	5.60

So take the data in the shaded area for example. On March 4, 2016, at
4:00pm EST, if you spend $3.80 to buy a call option of PFE, then you can
purchase one share of the PFE stock on or before January 19, 2018 at a price
of $28 per share. This is what you call "exercising the option."

Baroque Omaha: So how do I make a profit?

Professor Dong: If, on or before January 19, 2018, there is a moment in
which the stock price of PFE is higher than $28, you would want to exercise
the option and buy the stock at $28. You would then actually be paying less
than what the players in the market would need to pay.

Stilleven Jobs: What if I do not want to hold the stock?

Professor Dong: If you do not want to buy the stock at $28 for some reason, you can still sell the option and make a profit if, on or before January 19, 2018, there is a moment in which the stock price of PFE is significantly higher than $28. In fact financial theory has proved that it is almost always better to sell an option rather than to exercise it early.

Wanna Buffet: Okay, so what is a put option?

Professor Dong: Put option is an asset that, once you have purchased it, gives you the privilege to sell its corresponding asset at the pre-determined price in the future. Yet, you do not have any obligation to exercise this privilege.

For example, say you spend $1 to purchase an American put option on March 1, 2016. The option corresponds to the crude oil ETF (NYSE: OIL). The exercise price (also called strike price) is $45 and it expires on January 20, 2017.

This means that on or before January 20, 2017, you can sell one share of OIL at the price of $45 per share. If it is a European option, then you only have the right to sell one share of OIL at the price of $45 per share on January 20, 2017, but no sooner.

So on January 20, 2017, if the price of the OIL stock is lower than $45, you would want to exercise your put option and sell the ETF at the exercise price of $45.

Baroque Omaha: Why do I want to sell it at $45? I do not have OIL at hand. How do I sell something that I do not have?

Professor Dong: As we introduced in Chapter Five, you can still short sell an asset even if you never held it. The theoretical mechanism is that you borrow the asset from the broker, sell it at a high price, and wait for the price of the asset to decrease.

Then you enter the market and buy it back at a lower price. In reality, you do not need to go through this process step by step. Simply click on "sell" on a trading platform, and if the price of the asset goes down, your account balance will show a profit.

If the OIL price per share is lower than $45, you would want to exercise the put option and sell OIL at a price of $45. This way you receive the profit equal to the difference between $45 and the market price. You realize a profit because you can sell something at a higher price than others can.

Moselle Omaha: What if on January 20, 2017, the price of the OIL ETF is higher than $45?

Professor Dong: Then you simply do not exercise your put option and instead let it expire. In this case, you lose your initial cost of buying the put option, which is $1.

Moselle Omaha: What if the price of the OIL ETF is between $45 and $44?

Professor Dong: Good question. You would still want to exercise your option. For example, say that on January 20, 2017, the stock price is $44.6. If you exercise the option to sell the ETF at $45, and then you immediately buy it back at $44.6, you make $0.40 profit. This helps reduce your cost of buying the put option to just $0.60. If you do not exercise your put option, your loss would be $1: the entire cost of buying the put option.

Stilleven Jobs: So buying a put option is like buying insurance?

Professor Dong: Exactly. The cost of a put option is similar to the price of insurance for the seller. A seller holding a put option is guaranteed to be able to sell an asset at the put option's strike price. If the market of the underlying asset declines, the seller can still receive higher selling revenue. Typically insurance would bring payoff when things go bad. A put option brings profit when the asset price decreases so it is like an asset performance insurance.

Wanna Buffet: Can you also give an example of a put option?

Professor Dong:

Call option bid price	Call option ask price	Exercise Price	Put option bid price	Put option ask price
Expires on March 18, 2016				
0.84	0.95	29	0.16	0.18
0.49	0.56	29.5	0.29	0.34
0.26	0.29	30	0.52	0.58
0.09	0.13	30.5	0.86	0.94
Expires on December 16, 2016				
5.00	5.30	25	0.85	0.90
3.40	4.05	27	1.38	1.43
1.78	1.84	30	2.66	2.73
1.00	1.06	32	3.90	4.00
Expires on January 19, 2018				
5.50	5.75	25	1.97	2.05
3.60	3.80	28	3.15	3.35
2.62	2.76	30	4.15	4.35
1.85	1.97	32	5.35	5.60

Let's use the price table again. The price of the common stock Pfizer (NYSE: PFE) as of March 4, 2016, 4:00pm EST was $29.71. Some of its corresponding call and put option prices are listed in the table above.

On March 4, 2016, at 4:00pm EST, if you spend $3.35 to buy a put option of PFE, then you can sell one share of the PFE stock on or before January 19, 2018 at a price of $28 per share.

If on or before January 19, 2018, the price of PFE per share is at some moment lower than $28, then you can either sell the put option or exercise it and realize a gross profit.

Stilleven Jobs: Can you give a summary of the profit and loss of call and put options?

Professor Dong: Sure. The figures below represent the relationships between the net profit of different options and their underlying asset prices. The X in the figure is the exercise price of the option.

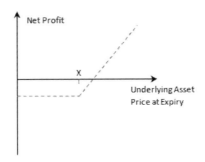

The above is the relationship between the net profit of buying a call option and the underlying asset price. The profit is negative and unchanged when the price of the asset is lower than the exercise price of the call option. However, the profit starts to grow when the price of the underlying asset becomes higher than the exercise price. The gain is unlimited, yet the loss is limited to the cost of the call option.

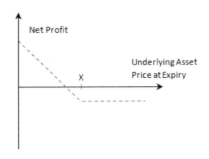

The chart above demonstrates the relationship between the net profit of buying a put option and the underlying asset price. The profit is higher when the price of the asset is lower than the exercise price of the put option. However, the profit is negative when the price of the underlying asset is higher than the exercise. The gain is limited[11], and the loss is limited to the cost of the put option.

Option transactions are zero-sum games. This implies that the profit from buying an option equates to the loss of the seller of the option.

On the other hand, the seller of option realizes profit when the buyers cannot exercise the option at hand[12]. Therefore, the relationships between net profit of selling options and the underlying asset price are as follows, for selling call and put options respectively.

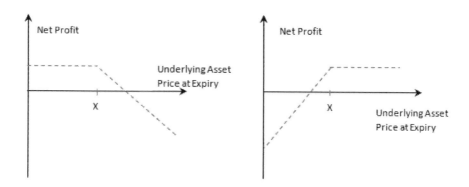

Compared to holding options, direct investment in assets can have a much greater, or even unlimited, loss. Options, however, can significantly hedge such a sizable loss. The loss on the position of the underlying asset will not go beyond the cost of options. Thus the maximum loss does not involve uncertainty.

Before we explore more about risk management strategies, we also need to understand the relationship between the net profit of direct investment in the underlying asset and the price of the underlying asset. The figures below represent such a relationship between long and short term assets respectively. The X in these cases stands for the price of the asset when the investor opens the long or short position. The illustration ignores the transaction costs of direct investments.

---

[11] It is limited to the extent that the underlying asset price can at the most decline to zero.

[12] It is widely believed, though lack of accurate source of empirical study, that 80% of the options end up expiring without any value. Only 20% of the options are exercised with a profit.

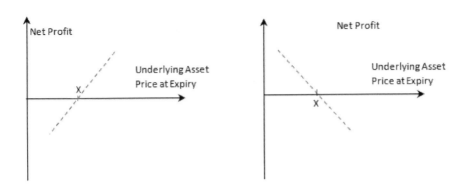

Wanna Buffet: I am more interested in how to use these options in my investments. Can you lay out some strategies?

Professor Dong: Yes, for pure option investments without combining them with their underlying assets, the strategies are as follows.

If you believe that an underlying asset, whether it is a stock or an ETF, has a higher likelihood to appreciate than to depreciate, you should consider three strategies: taking a long position on the asset, taking a long position on its call option, or taking a short position on its put option.

If the asset is less volatile and pays a good dividend, directly taking a long position of the asset is the best strategy. If the asset is very volatile and pays a low dividend or none at all, taking a long call option works the best. If you firmly believe that the asset price has a very limited downside and does not have the potential to increase, taking a short put option is ideal.

Likewise, if you believe the price of the underlying asset is more likely to decrease rather than increase, you should consider the other three strategies: taking a short position on the asset, taking a long position on its put option, or taking a short position on its call option.

If the asset price is less volatile, taking a short position on the asset directly is the best choice. If the asset is volatile and the chance of price appreciation is not trivial, it is then recommended to buy a put option for the asset.

If the asset price is very likely to decrease, yet it would not decrease very significantly, you might consider selling its call option if you believe its chance of price appreciation is very low.

Baroque Omaha: Can you share the reasoning for these strategies?

Professor Dong: Of course. For a stock or ETF whose price would more likely increase, you can buy it directly. Buying its call option can also capture the price appreciation and it can hedge the risk. Yet if the asset price is not volatile, meaning it will not likely go down dramatically, then buying its call option becomes unnecessary.

By selling its put option, you can receive the selling proceeds immediately and reinvest such revenue. As long as the price does not go down, you get to keep the income you gain from selling the put option.

However, if the asset price does decrease, your revenue will decline and eventually become negative, which is your loss. Such a loss can be very significant depending on the degree at which the asset price decreases to zero.

On the other hand, if you believe that the asset price would more likely decrease, you can directly short the asset to make a profit. But if the asset price is volatile, its chance of going up is high and the direct short strategy might be risky.

Buying its put option in this case can limit your loss in case the asset price rallies. Selling its call option can bring you the revenue if the asset price remains low. However, this is a *very* risky strategy; if the asset price increases, you will incur unlimited loss.

Moselle Omaha: Why don't we just use options to substitute the entire direct long or short positions? Is there a downside to this strategy?

Professor Dong: Yes, options have their limits and you should only start to use one when you become a more experienced investor. Even professional investors treat options very carefully because they realize the risks involved in them.

First, options bring less of a profit than direct positions. Buying a call option will help to realize profit when the asset price goes up, but such a profit is less than that which would come from directly buying the asset, because you need to pay the call option's cost. The same reasoning applies to put options. The trade-off is the protection you receive if the asset price moves oppositely.

Second, options will expire. The time value of options decreases day by day as you purchase and hold them. If you buy a call option of a stock or ETF because you believe its price will increase, you might still incur the loss equal to the cost of purchasing the asset, if the asset price only increases after your option expires.

Thirdly, options are highly leveraged. The market common practice of option purchasing is round-lot based. This implies that you must buy multiplications of 100 shares of an option, for example, 100, 300, or 1500. These option positions correspond to the number of underlying assets.

For example, the price is $5 for one share of a call option for the J.P. Morgan stock (NYSE: JPM) at the exercise price of $40. At expiry, if the JPM price is $48 per share, your gross profit is $800 and your cost is $500. Yet if the JPM price is less than $40 at expiration, your cost of buying the call option, which is $500, becomes a complete loss.

Fourth, options are not available for some assets, and some options are not liquid. There are many stocks and some ETFs that do not have a parallel options market. Some stocks, that are likely illiquid *per se*, have an option market that is even less liquid. The bid-ask spread of the option is too wide to make a transaction profitable.

Wanna Buffet: You mentioned that there are also combined option strategies?

Professor Dong: Yes. Long positions of call or put options, or short positions of call or put, are called "pure option strategies". There are combined strategies that involve more than one option. I would like to introduce the following: covered call, protective put, straddles, strangles, spread, butterflies, and condors.

Stilleven Jobs: What is a covered call?

Professor Dong: A covered call is a strategy in which you buy an asset and sell its call option. So when the asset price goes down, you incur a loss by holding the asset but you gain some revenue by selling its call option; when the asset price goes up, your asset position realizes a profit, yet you will need to accept that the buyer of your call option may exercise it against you.

Baroque Omaha: So what's the point of using this covered call strategy?

Professor Dong: I would like to quote a widely-cited, practical and precise explanation, from Tradeking.com:
"When you sell covered calls, you're usually hoping to keep your shares of the underlying stock while generating extra income via the option premium. You'll want the stock price to remain below your strike price, so the option buyer won't be motivated to exercise the option and grab your shares away from you. That way, the options will expire worthless, you'll keep the entire option premium at expiration and you'll also keep your shares of the underlying stock."
"If your stock's price is neutral or dropping a bit, but you still want to hold onto the shares longer-term, writing covered calls can be a good way to earn extra income on your long position. But remember, you're also a stockholder, so you'll most likely want the value of your shares to increase – just not enough to hit your covered call's strike price. Then you won't just keep the premium from the options sale, you'll also benefit from the shares' rise in value."
"Imagine you already own 100 shares of XYZ. You bought them for $25 each, plus the commission of $4.95, and now XYZ is trading at $50 - but it doesn't seem likely to increase much in the short-term. Still, you're long-term bullish on XYZ and want to see if you can make a little extra cash while waiting for a bigger bump in the stock. In January, you sell one covered call

contract on XYZ. Let's say the option you've sold has March expiration and a strike price of 55. The premium you collect is $2.50 per option, or $250 ($2.50 x 100 shares = $250) less commissions of $5.60."

"If XYZ stays around $50 until [the] March expiration, the call would be out-of-the-money. That means buying the stock for the strike price ($55) is more expensive than buying the stock in the open market ($50). So the option buyer would most likely not exercise the call and the option would expire worthless. You pocket the $250 premium AND keep your 100 shares of XYZ. Keep in mind, as long as the options you sell don't get exercised, you can repeat this maneuver from month to month, selling additional covered calls against the same shares of stock."

Moselle Omaha: What is a "protective put?"

Professor Dong: When you hold a long position for an asset and also buy its put option, you are holding a protective put. The put option will bring profit if the asset price goes down, and the long position of the asset will bring profit if the asset appreciates.

Therefore, the relationship between net profit and asset price for a protective put is similar to such a relationship for the long position of a call option. Of course, a long call position is most likely a lot cheaper than a protective put.

Baroque Omaha: So why do we still use a protective put strategy, since it is the same as a call option but is less cost effective?

Professor Dong: Well, investors do not always have the luxury of picking an investment strategy from the beginning. When they are forced to receive an asset, they have already missed the opportunity to utilize its call option as a substitution.

The most straightforward way to hedge the downside risk after they hold an asset is to buy its put option.

For example, your employer might grant you some stocks in your company, or you might receive some stocks as a gift or inheritance. In these cases, you can use a put option as price insurance to hedge the risk of price decline after you have already received the long position of the asset.

In addition, a protective put is not exactly the same as a call. The former receives dividends because you are holding the underlying asset; the latter does not bring any dividend income.

Baroque Omaha: What is a straddle?

Professor Dong: Typically, a straddle is to buy a call and a put option at the same exercise price. So whether the asset price was low or high, this strategy would realize a profit. Yet if the asset price was less volatile, this strategy would bring a loss.

The worst case scenario would be if the asset price remained the same as the exercise price of the call and the put options. In this case the holder of the straddle would lose all the cost of buying the call and the put.

Typically, the purchase and sell of a straddle requires the same commission, as if it is a single option. The relationship between the net profit and the price of the underlying asset can be described in the following chart:

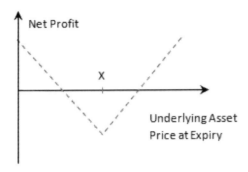

Stilleven Jobs: What are the benefits and limits of a straddle?

Professor Dong: A straddle changes the goal of the investment. For direct investments on assets, investors take their best estimate in terms of the direction of asset price: whether it is going to increase or decrease. For a straddle, investors focus more on the asset volatility rather than asset price direction. Asset volatilities are easier to predict in general.

A straddle, however, can be expensive and the tradeoff time between to expiration and cost exists. The longer the time to expiration the more likely the straddle can be profitable - yet it is also more expensive. So if the straddle does not bring a profit, the loss, in the extreme case, can be very high.

Wanna Buffet: I heard that there are some different kinds of straddles. What are they?

Professor Dong: Good question. If you buy two call options and one put option at the same exercise price, you will receive more of a profit when the asset price appreciates. This applies to the case in which the asset has a significantly higher chance of realizing a higher price in the future. Such a strategy is called a strap.

However, if the asset price is not volatile enough, it is then very risky to apply this trading logic, as the holder might end up not exercising any option and instead incur a sizable loss.

On the other hand, if you buy two put options and one call option at the same exercise price, you will receive more of a profit when the asset price depreciates. This is called a strip. Again, while this strategy has the nice nature of receiving a profit either way, it relies on the high volatility of the underlying asset. Furthermore, the cost of call and put options are positively related to the volatility of the underlying asset. This implies that it is not a feasible strategy to pursue very volatile underlying assets to improve the chance of paying off the option cost and realizing profit. With the increase of asset volatility, investors would find it is more difficult to make up the option cost.

The following figures present the net profit-asset price relationship for a strap and a strip respectively:

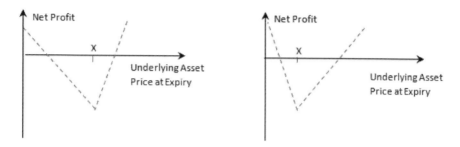

Moselle Omaha: What is a strangle?

Professor Dong: A strangle is similar to a straddle but has a lower potential of profit and loss. A strangle consists of buying a call option at a higher exercise price and a put option at a lower exercise price. Therefore the call and put options are less likely to be exercised. This would make the options less expensive, so the potential loss would also be less severe. The following figure presents the net profit-asset price relationship for a strangle:

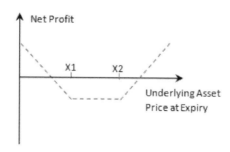

In a nutshell, a strangle can be a powerful instrument for volatile assets whose options have longer periods before expiration. Investors do not need to forecast the direction in which the price is moving, but instead must simply forecast the volatility of the underlying asset. Compared to straddles, strangles have less profit and less loss.

Baroque Omaha: What is a spread?

Professor Dong: There are two types of spreads: bullish and bearish. Their net profit-asset price relationships are presented as follows, respectively.

A bullish spread, as the first figure shows, generates positive returns when the underlying asset price increases and incurs loss when the asset price decreases. The gain and the loss are capped.

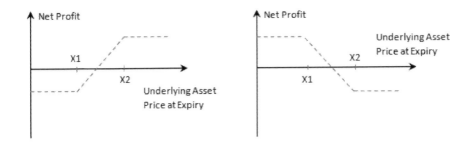

A bullish spread can be assembled by simultaneously buying a call option at a lower exercise price and selling a call option at a higher exercise price. This can reduce the cost of simply buying a call option. However, this sacrifices the unlimited potential of profit.

Therefore, a bullish spread can be appropriate for options that are closer to expiry or underlying assets that are not volatile. In these cases, foregoing the unlimited profit potential does not mean a significant compromise, because the likelihood of large price increase is not material when the options are close to expiration *per se*. At the meantime, the cost of a spread is no higher than a single option.

A bearish spread, on the other hand, brings gain when the asset price decreases. If the underlying asset price goes up, a bullish spread will incur loss for its holder.

A bearish spread can be assembled by simultaneously buying a put option at a higher exercise price and selling a put option at lower exercise price. This can reduce the cost of simply buying a put option.

However, this again sacrifices the potential for a sizable profit. Likewise, a bearish spread rather than a put option is more appropriate for assets whose downsides are not significant.

Stilleven Jobs: What is a butterfly?

Professor Dong: A butterfly assembled by call options is implemented by simultaneously buying a call option at a lower exercise price, buying a call option at a higher exercise price, and selling two shares of call options at exercise prices right in the middle.

The following figure shows how the butterfly strategy is set up.

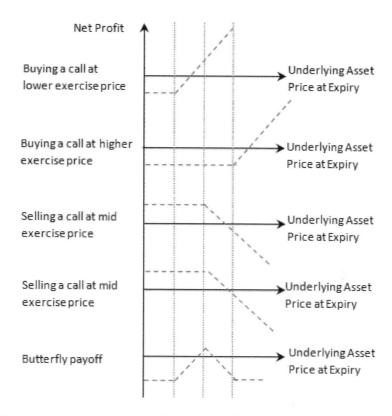

The butterfly strategy is similar to the bullish or bearish strategies in the sense that it gains profit if the underlying asset is not volatile. However, butterfly holders do not need to pick a side; they are not concerned about if the underlying asset will appreciate or depreciate.

A butterfly would be a good strategy, as long as the asset is not volatile or the options are close to expiry so that the chance of asset price moving out of the "tip" of the payoff curve is low.

On the other hand, if the underlying asset price can be volatile before the expiry of options, an iron butterfly strategy might be beneficial. An iron butterfly is a combination of buying two call options at the exercise price in the middle, and selling two call options, one at a high exercise price and one at a low exercise price.

Apparently, the iron butterfly strategy carries the benefit of side-independence. Its holder does not need to make a correct forecast in terms of the asset price's moving direction. However, its upside is limited and if the asset price is not volatile, the investor will incur a loss.

The payoff curve of an iron butterfly strategy is:

Wanna Buffet: What is a condor?

Professor Dong: A condor can be understood as simultaneously buying a strangle that has a narrower range and selling a strangle that has a wider range. Specifically, a condor strategy means to sell a call at a low exercise price (X2), to buy a call at an even lower exercise price (X1), to sell a call at a high exercise price (X3), and to buy a call at an even higher exercise price (X4). The payoff illustration is presented with the iron condor.

A condor, obviously, can be compared to a butterfly, but has a wider chance of realizing profit. When the underlying asset is not likely to be volatile before the options expire, a condor is beneficial to its holder.

The cost of a higher chance of profit is the lower magnitude of profit. In addition, condors carry a lower cost and thus a lower loss if the asset price becomes significantly high or low.

Baroque Omaha: What is an iron condor?

Professor Dong: An iron condor has the opposite payoff of a condor. To set up an iron condor, investors buy a call at a low exercise price (X2), sell a call at an even lower exercise price (X1), buy a call at a high exercise price (X3), and sell a call at an even higher exercise price (X4).

In fact, when investors initially trade a condor or iron condor, they do not need to manually buy and sell four different options. Trading software, platforms, or apps usually have the function of directly inputting the parameters of a condor and investing with the strategy through one single purchase.

The payoff of an iron condor in terms of the price of the underlying asset is described in the following figure. An iron condor is a low cost and low loss strategy for investors who do not have "side bias," with the tradeoff of lower and limited profit potential, compared to the iron butterfly.

If an investor does not have expectations in terms of the direction in which the asset price will move, an iron condor might still bring the investor some profit, as long as the price of the underlying asset is volatile enough before the options expire.

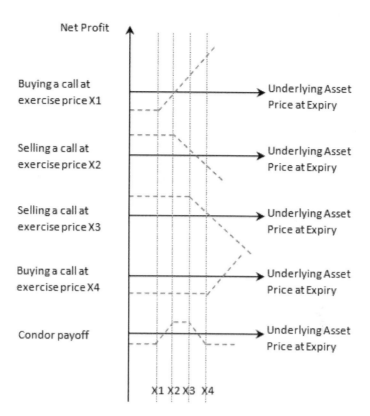

There is a tradeoff between the width of the iron condor and the loss. If the span of the condor is wide, the chance of realizing profit is low, but the loss is also lower. On the other hand, if the span of the condor is narrow, the chance of realizing a profitable iron condor is large. However, if the strategy still ends up falling into the loss zone given such a high chance of profit, the loss can be significant. As the options move close to expiry, the likelihood of the asset price moving outside of the loss zone decreases.

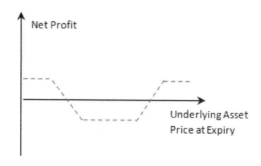

Baroque Omaha: So overall, can we conclude that investing in options only brings limited exposure to loss as opposed to directly investing in assets?

Professor Dong: Not necessarily. Options can be used to hedge risk when you have already invested in the underlying assets. Options can also be used as alternative investment vehicles to gain exposure to risk and return.

However, it is not correct to assert that holding options have lower risks than the act of directly holding their underlying assets. Options are in fact more leveraged and might involve a greater loss than the direct holding of underlying assets.

The nature of the limited time for options increases the risk of such a loss. The price volatility of assets can lead to a greater return volatility of options.

Here is a fictional comprehensive example, using the Walmart stock (NYSE: WMT) as the underlying asset and ignoring the transaction cost. The example considers four different scenarios: large asset gain, minimal asset gain, zero gain, and minimal asset loss.

Obviously, when there is a loss, direct holding an asset will incur more loss in terms of dollar value, and the use of options for assets will incur a higher loss rate yet a lower dollar value loss.

Direct purchase of 100 shares of WMT on March 24, 2016 at $68 per share	Investing in 100 shares of WMT call option on March 24, 2016 at $1.59 per share, exercise price: $68, expiration: May 6, 2016
Cost: $6800	Cost: $159
On May 6, 2016, sell 100 shares of WMT at $70 per share	On May 6, 2016, WMT stock price is $70, so the investor exercises the call option
Profit: $200	**Profit: $41**
Return rate: 2.9412%	**Return rate: 25.7862%**

Direct purchase of 100 shares of WMT on March 24, 2016 at $68 per share	Investing in 100 shares of WMT call option on March 24, 2016 at $1.59 per share, exercise price: $68, expiration: May 6, 2016
Cost: $6800	Cost: $159
On May 6, 2016, sell 100 shares of WMT at $69 per share	On May 6, 2016, WMT stock price is $69, so the investor exercises the call option
Profit: $100	**Profit: -$59**
Return rate: 1.4706%	**Return rate: -37.1069%**

Direct purchase of 100 shares of	Investing in 100 shares of WMT call

WMT on March 24, 2016 at $68 per share Cost: $6800 On May 6, 2016, sell 100 shares of WMT at $68 per share **Profit: $0** **Return rate: 0%**	option on March 24, 2016 at $1.59 per share, exercise price: $68, expiration: May 6, 2016 Cost: $159 On May 6, 2016, WMT stock price is $68, so the call option expires at no value **Profit: $-159** **Return rate: -100%**
Direct purchase of 100 shares of WMT on March 24, 2016 at $68 per share Cost: $6800 On May 6, 2016, sell 100 shares of WMT at $34 per share **Profit: $-3400** **Return rate: -50%**	Investing in 100 shares of WMT call option on March 24, 2016 at $1.59 per share, exercise price: $68, expiration: May 6, 2016 Cost: $159 On May 6, 2016, WMT stock price is $34, so the call option expires at no value **Profit: -$159** **Return rate: -100%**

This in fact implies that option is more leveraged. It could produce greater gains or losses with lower amount of capital input.

Wanna Buffet: I hear the word "leverage" here and there in finance. I never really understand what it means. What you explain it?

Professor Dong: Yes. The word leverage comes from physics, implying that you can move something heavy with little force by using a lever, like the picture[13] shows below.

---

[13] Cited from study.com

In finance, leverage means that an investor could spend fewer amounts of initial capital inputs to generate greater gains or losses by borrowing capital from the brokerage companies or third parties. In business, leverage means that a firm borrows capital by issuing bonds or using other liabilities to gain control of greater scale of assets.

Stilleven Jobs: Are we all done?

Professor Dong: Not yet. I would like to give you a roadmap of *Volume One*.

Chapter one introduced how to use the interviews.

Chapter two discussed the Exchange-Trade Funds (ETF), which are the most important investable assets that non-professional investors should begin with.

Chapter three introduced all the possible financial assets and analyzed their risk-return features.

Chapter four disclosed some hidden facts about funds and professional investment services to conclude that investors should invest by themselves.

Chapter five set up the foundation of investments by introducing concepts, jargons, and calculations.

Chapter six presented the risk-return rewarding relationship, and taught investors how to plan their investment targets by computing the risks of assets.

Chapter seven introduced investment strategies and styles for different types of investors and different purposes of investments.

Chapter eight analyzed in detail the reasons of buy and sell, position control, investment timing, and common errors made by investors because of the psychological factors.

Chapter nine clarified the common misunderstandings of diversification by introducing correct methods of portfolio risk management.

Chapter ten introduced options, which are assets that can be used for stand-alone investments, as well as risk control instruments that can be blended with other assets.

Overall, *Volume One* gives you the complete picture of investments, without going to the details of individual asset selection skills. We will learn those in *Volume Two*.

Baroque Omaha: What is covered in Volume Two then? How to pick stocks?

Professor Dong: Yes, and much more than that. *Volume two* introduces stock selection methods systematically by going through three layers: macro-environment; industry characteristics; and individual company investment analyses.

Volume Two then moves on to discuss in detail the third most significant reason[14] of investment failure, which is the psychological biases and irrationality of investors.

Volume Two also introduces the financial instruments that can be used to diversity the equity portfolio and reduce risk. These instruments include international equities, bonds, and alternative assets.

---

[14] The most significant reason of investment failure is of course the incorrect selection of investment asset; the second most is the wrong timing of buying and selling the asset, even though it is correctly selected.

ABOUT THE AUTHOR

Professor Huijian Dong earned his Ph. D. in Financial Economics from the University of Delaware. He then took the appointment at Pacific University (Oregon, USA) as a finance faculty. There he co-founded the Master of Science in Finance program, the MBA program, and the finance concentration at the undergraduate level. He earned the Chartered Financial Analyst (CFA) designation in 2015. He actively serves in various executive roles in mutual funds and financial advising companies in the United States and China. He served as a senior manager at New Oriental Group (NYSE: EDU) before he moved to the U. S.

Students usually remark that his lectures are easy to chew, reliable in the long term, and practical in real life. He has been invited frequently as an advisor and guest speaker for well-known investment luncheons, universities, and capital management forums, both in the U.S. and in China.

He can be reached at prof.dong@outlook.com.

Made in the USA
San Bernardino, CA
13 July 2016